THEMES
for early years

WEATHER

LINDA MORT & JANET MORRIS

THEMES
for early years

Authors Linda Mort and Janet Morris
Editor Jane Bishop
Assistant editor Sally Gray
Series designer Lynne Joesbury
Designer Louise Belcher
Illustrations Chris Russell
Cover Lynne Joesbury
Action Rhymes, Poems and Stories compiled by Jackie Andrews
Songs compiled by Peter Morrell
Assemblies chapter by Lesley Prior
To the children, staff and parents of Early Years Nursery School, Manchester
Designed using Adobe Pagemaker
Processed by Scholastic Ltd, Leamington Spa

Published by Scholastic Ltd, Villiers House, Clarendon Avenue, Leamington Spa, Warwickshire CV32 5PR
© 1997 Scholastic Ltd Text © 1997 Linda Mort and Janet Morris
2 3 4 5 6 7 8 9   7 8 9 0 1 2 3 4 5
The publishers gratefully acknowledge permission to reproduce the following copyright material:
Jill Atkins for 'Jack Frost' © 1997, Jill Atkins; Clive Barnwell for 'Blow Wind Blow' © 1997, Clive Barnwell and 'Just Like The Birds
Do' © 1997, Clive Barnwell; Sue Cowling for 'Weather House' and 'Wind Farm' © 1997, Sue Cowling; John Foster for 'It's Snowed'
© 1997, John Foster; 'Keeping Cool' © 1997, John Foster; 'The Shirts On The Line' from *You Little Monkey and other Poems* by
John Foster © 1996, John Foster (1996, Oxford University Press).'Ten White Snowmen' from *Snow Poems* Ed. John Foster © 1990,
John Foster (1990, Oxford University Press) and 'What Is Fog?' from *Language In Colour* Ed. Moira Andrew © 1989, John Foster
(1989, Belair); Jean Gilbert for 'Snowy Footprints' and 'Summertime' © 1997, Jean Gilbert; Carole Henderson-Begg for 'Splish,
Splash' © 1997, Carole Henderson-Begg; Hazel Hobbs for 'Sunshine Calypso' © 1997, Hazel Hobbs; Jan Holdstock for 'When The
Blue Skies Turn to Grey' and 'Safe Sun' © 1997, Jan Holdstock; Jan Jones for 'If I Was A Raindrop' © 1997, Jan Jones; Karen King
for 'Leroy's Rainbow' © 1997, Karen King; Tony Mitton for 'Getting Dressed For Winter' © 1997, Tony Mitton; 'Fog' © 1997, Tony
Mitton; 'Can You Feel The Beat' © 1997, Tony Mitton; 'The Sail Song' © 1997, Tony Mitton and 'Hibernating Hedgehog' previously
published in *Child Education* magazine (Scholastic Limited); Linda Mort and Janet Morris for 'Rainbow Rhyme' © 1997, Linda Mort
and Janet Morris and 'A Brave Boy', an adaptation of the story 'The Leak in the Dyke' by Mary Dodge (1965) © 1997, Linda Mort
and Janet Morris and 'A Brave Girl' © 1997, Linda Mort and Janet Morris; Judith Nicholls for 'Going, Going Gone' © 1997, Judith
Nicholls; Sue Nicholls for 'A Foggy Day' © 1997, Sue Nicholls and 'A Rainbow' © 1997, Sue Nicholls; Sue Palmer for 'The Colours
Of The Rainbow' first published in *English Through Topics: Weather KS1 Teachers' Notes* © 1993, Sue Palmer (1993, Longman);
Lesley Prior for three assemblies © 1997, Lesley Prior; Scholastic Ltd for the use of text from *The Foggy Day* by John Cunnliffe, ©
1984, John Cunnliffe (1996, Andre Deutsch); Susheila Stone for the second version of 'Storm Song' © 1997 Susheila Storm.
Every effort has been made to trace copyright holders and the publishers apologise for any inadvertent omissions.

British Library Cataloguing-in-Publication Data A catalogue record for this book is available from the British Library.

ISBN 0-590-53683-4

CONTENTS

INTRODUCTION

Children are fascinated with all aspects of the weather. They hear their parents and teachers talk about the weather almost daily, and, to young children, the weather can appear to have mysterious, magical and awesome qualities, over which even adults have no control.

As a theme 'the weather' provides an all-encompassing range of topics for early years' practitioners. It can provide many and varied opportunities to introduce young children, whether at home, in playgroup, nursery or reception class, to concepts about the weather in stimulating ways which will appeal to their need for first hand experiences and opportunities for active learning.

Throughout this book the emphasis is on encouraging children's observation and language skills. Through such an approach, young children can make their own 'connections' between different areas of the curriculum, relating their developing knowledge and understanding of different aspects of the weather with personal experiences in their own lives.

LOOKING AT WEATHER

Each chapter of the book focuses on a different kind of weather. Chapter 1 (Sun) provides opportunities for structured play situations, sand play and a look at sunflowers. In Chapter 2 (Rain) the children can sing the rhyme 'Incy Wincy Spider', make and use a rain gauge, test dolls' capes for waterproofness, learn about the rain forests, produce 'stormy' sounds with percussion instruments, and use real raindrops to create 'rainy' pictures.

In Chapter 3 (Wind), children experience the 'pull' of the wind through the use of balloons, they can make wind chimes and design kites, windmills and weather vanes. They can sail boats outside on a windy day, and learn about Grace Darling's bravery on a windswept sea. Chapter 4 (Clouds and fog) provides ideas which enable children to see 'raindrops' being formed in a 'cloud', and to make their own cloud mobiles. They can learn that fog is 'low cloud' and about the dangers of 'smog'. Through structured play, children learn about traffic pollution and what can be done about it and also about the problems caused by fog for farmers and drivers. In Chapter 5 (Snow and ice), children investigate frozen puddles and indoor 'icebergs', and explore the properties of snow. They can pretend to be animals hibernating in the snow, and even dramatise Scott's expedition to Antarctica!

In Chapter 6 (The effects of the weather) activities take the children on a world-wide trip to find out about how the weather affects people, animals and sports events.

HOW TO USE THIS BOOK

Themes for early years – Weather is one of a series of books written for early years' educators of children aged between three and six years.

To help children of this age learn it is vital to be constantly attuned to their responses to their own environment. It is also important to be highly imaginative and resourceful in order to gain, and sustain children's attention, without in any way cramping their style or repressing their spontaneity and curiosity.

Pre-school children learn best when they have plenty of opportunity and space to use their bodies and all five senses. They also need access to adults who will listen and respond sensitively to their questions and observations. This makes it exacting but highly rewarding work. This book aims to assist early years' educators to help children learn about the weather with a range of workable ideas and resources appropriate to young children's needs and interests.

However you choose to use the material you can adjust the activities and resources to suit the needs of the children within your care.

TOPIC WEB

The diagram on pages 8–9, which may be photocopied, is to assist you in planning a series of activities for a week, a month or a term. This topic web relates all the activities in the book to the subject areas of the National Curriculum and the Scottish 5–14 Guidelines.

ACTIVITY PAGES

Each chapter in the book looks at a specific type of weather and provides a series of activities to investigate the theme. There is a single activity per page and each is laid out in an identical manner for ease of use.

First a learning objective is established showing the main curriculum area covered, together with a summary of what the children will be doing. Next the ideal group size is indicated, a list of items needed to complete the task is provided and any necessary preparation is explained. In 'What to do', step-by-step instructions describe the main activity. Important discussion areas are then highlighted and finally some follow-up suggestions are given.

DISPLAYS

A display of the children's work can involve them both in setting it up and in interactive activities once it is established. Display can also provide an important way of keeping parents and visitors informed about the activities taking place in the playgroup, nursery or reception class. In this section some specific ideas for displays based on activities in the earlier chapters are described and illustrated.

ASSEMBLIES

Your group may be multi-cultural with different forms of worship which can be shared and experienced. This chapter provides specific ideas for assemblies or group sharing times based on the theme of weather. Each assembly has its own practical ideas on how the children can be encouraged to contribute and reflect on a theme. with recommendations for songs and prayers.

RESOURCES

A useful selection of stories, songs, poems and action rhymes on the theme of the weather is provided. Many are directly referred to in the activity pages. Much of this material has been commissioned to suit the topic and all the pages in this section may be photocopied.

PHOTOCOPIABLE SHEETS

There are eight photocopiable pages each related to a previous activity in the book and providing a task for the children to undertake. Make sure they are clear what their task is and that any new vocabulary is explained before they start.

RECOMMENDED MATERIALS

The final page in the book provides a list of useful, additional resource material in the form of story books, information books, song and poetry books, audio cassette tapes and other teaching items.

EXPRESSIVE ARTS

Planning towards the National Curriculum and the Scottish National guidelines 5-14

PREPARING FOR PRIMARY SCHOOL

THE NATIONAL CURRICULUM

A National Curriculum was established to ensure that all schools teach the same subject for the same amount of time each week, so that any child moving to another part of the country is not disadvantaged. National Curriculum subjects are: English, Mathematics, Science, History, Geography, Design and Technology, Information Technology, RE, Art, Music and PE.

Children begin work under the guidelines of the National Curriculum at the start of compulsory schooling (the term after a child's fifth birthday). Before this, every child's experiences will vary but it is essential that the curriculum they experience beforehand is child-based and not subject-based. This means essentially a play-based curriculum, with a great emphasis on sensory learning, discussion and physical activity.

TOWARDS LEVEL ONE

Before compulsory school, children are working towards Level One and it is the play-based curriculum which informs the rationale of the activities in this book. Each activity has a learning

objective which is related to a subject area of the National Curriculum, but which is achieved through play based activities. In this way, the *Desirable Outcomes for Children's Learning on entering compulsory education* prescribed by the School Curriculum and Assessment Authority may be achieved in developmentally appropriate ways. The *Desirable Outcomes for Children's Learning* are divided into six main areas – personal and social development, language and literacy, mathematics, knowledge and understanding of the world, physical development and creative development. These areas of learning all lead into the National Curriculum subjects and can be taught to young children through varied and imaginative play experiences of the kind to be found in this book.

THE SCOTTISH NATIONAL GUIDELINES 5–14

In Scotland, there are National Guidelines for schools on what should be taught to children between the ages of five and fourteen.

These National Guidelines are divided into six main curriculum areas: English Language, Mathematics, Environmental Studies, Expressive Arts, Religious and Moral Education, Personal and Social Development.

Within these main areas, further subjects are found, for example, 'Expressive Arts' includes art and design, drama, music and PE. Strands are also identified within each subject, for example Mathematics includes problem-solving and enquiry, and shape, position and movement.

Most nurseries and playgroups will find that the experiences they are offering children will be laying a firm foundation for this curriculum. This book provides activities which will help prepare children for many aspects of it, and they will also fit well into the pre-five curriculum guidelines issued by local authorities throughout Scotland.

To help with your planning, the individual activities have been allocated to separate areas of the curriculum on the topic web on pages 8 and 9. The children's personal and social development is an on-going theme that is incorporated throughout the activities in the book.

CHAPTER 1 SUN

Through structured play children can 'buy' items for a summer holiday, recreate a beach scene, experience a taste of desert life in the sand tray, and keep flies at bay in their kitchen! They can make their own sun-hats, examine sunflowers, have fun with their shadows, and investigate the fading effect of sunlight with the activities in this chapter.

SUN SHOP

Objective

Mathematics – to 'buy' holiday items using numbers up to 10.

Group size

Up to six children.

What you need

A collection of money boxes, piggy-banks, purses and wallets. Sun lotions (including a waterproof version), 'After-sun' cream (all with lids secured with adhesive tape), nose shields and sun-block cream for lips. Sunglasses, sun-hats, swimsuits, trunks, towels, buckets, spades, beach balls, labels or card (for prices), a felt-tipped pen, pennies, shopping bags or baskets, play till.

Preparation

Set up a shop arranging two tables – one to display the items and one as a shop counter. Label the items with prices in pennies (up to 10p), and arrange them on a table. Arrange four chairs, side by side, at right angles to the display and counter. While one of the customers is being served, the others can watch and listen to the actions of the shopkeeper while they wait for their turn.

What to do

Use the shop for a role-play exercise letting the children and adults present take turns to buy and sell the products needed for a beach holiday.

Start the children off by showing them how to count out their pennies to buy the items. Reinforce any mathematical language, 'the sun-hat is two pennies more than the cream but the same price as the bucket'. Encourage them to play independently but join in where necessary to keep them going.

Discussion

Talk about how people save up money to buy things they need for a beach holiday. Show the children the money boxes, piggy-banks, purses and wallets, and ask the children if any of them are saving up for their holidays and, if so, what they might like to buy. Use the opportunity to reinforce the importance of using sun lotions, and the meaning of the words waterproof and protection. Ask why we need to wear sunglasses, reminding the children never to look directly at the sun even wearing sunglasses, and talk about why it is a good idea to wear a T-shirt in the sea, and on the beach.

Follow-up activities

✧ Let a doll use the shop. Pretend she has 5p to spend and let the children help her choose what she wants to buy.
✧ Use photocopiable page 88 and encourage the children to count out the correct number of pennies to match the items for sale.
✧ Sing the song 'Safe Sun' on page 87

COOL HEADS

Objective

Design and technology – to experiment with bending and folding different shapes of paper to make sun-hats.

Group size

Up to four children.

What you need

Examples or pictures of traditional sun-hats from around the world (a sombrero, a coolie hat, a child's legionnaire's hat, a Bedouin keffiyeh, a cricketer's hat, a baseball cap), sugar paper, scissors, adhesive tape, ribbon, a mirror.

Preparation

Cut the sugar paper into squares, rectangles, circles (see diagrams).

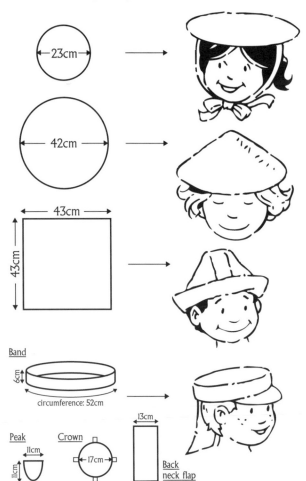

What to do

Gather the children together to look at the selection of hats available. Let them try them on and investigate them fully.

Now explain that they are going to make their own sun-hats out of paper. Provide the cut out shapes and let them experiment with bending, folding and sticking the sugar paper with adhesive tape, to create their own head protection.

On a sunny day, let the children admire their creations in the mirror, and then go outside in the sun to see if their hats do keep their heads cool!

Discussion

Talk about why we need to keep our heads covered in the sun, and what would happen if we did not (sunburn, sunstroke). Talk about how the sun 'beats' down on our heads, and read the poem 'Can you feel the beat?' on page 67. Examine the traditional hats, and the hats the children have made and talk about the different parts such as the peak and the brim. Consider whether the hats do keep all parts of the head and neck in the shade. Talk about what the sun-hats are made from, and why (straw, cotton). Would plastic or wool be suitable materials? Why not?

Follow-up activities

✧ Decorate the hats with ribbon and pieces of coloured tissue, and have a fashion show for the other children.

✧ Show a picture of an Australian outback hat (with dangling corks) and try making one using an old straw hat with holes punched around the brim. Show a picture of a bee-keeper's hat and make one using a piece of net curtain material.

✧ Can the children think what you could use if you didn't have a hat? Try a knotted handkerchief or a folded piece of newspaper for a quick sun-hat!

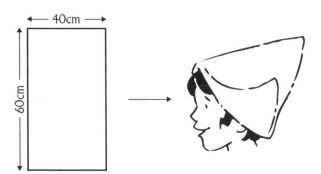

TRICKLY AND TICKLY

Objective

English – to describe the sensory experiences of a beach holiday.

Group size

Up to eight children.

What you need

A sheet of blue material or a plastic play cloth to represent the sea. Rubber rings, arm bands, dolls, beach balls, a baby bath or water play container, salt, a sheet of brown material to represent the beach, shells, shallow container of sand or nursery sand tray, towels, sun lotion, sunglasses, sun-hats. A tray containing cups of cold drinks, replica ice-lollies and ice-cream made from card and paper, card, felt-tipped pen, small table, postcards of beach scenes, *Where's Wally?* by Martin Handford (Walker Books), tambourine and sandpaper blocks.

Preparation

Set up an area as 'the sea' adjacent to the 'beach'. Set up a refreshments' stall on the beach, using a small table, and sign. Put a small amount of luke-warm water in the baby bath/water container set up on the floor.

What to do

Show the children the postcards of beach scenes and the beach page in *Where's Wally?* Discuss with the children the sights, sounds, textures, smells and tastes which they associate with a beach holiday. If possible let the children change into swimsuits and trunks, otherwise they can just take off their socks and shoes.

Let the children visit 'the beach' and 'the sea' and encourage them to dip their toes in the water and to wiggle them in the sand. Spread towels on the beach, and let everyone pretend they are on holiday. Let the children teach the dolls to 'swim' and put a tiny amount of sun lotion on themselves and the dolls. (Ensure that you limit the amount of sun lotion used and check with parents for any skin allergies or reactions.)

As the children play let them sing the song 'Summertime' on page 81, making all the appropriate sound effects.

Discussion

Focus the children's thoughts on words to describe their sensory experiences of the beach by playing this game called 'What can I?'. As the children play on the 'beach' or in the 'sea' ask them to say out loud (but not all at the same time): What can I see? What can I hear? What can I feel? What can I smell? What can I taste?

Follow-up activities

✧ Write down the words the children say when they play 'What can I?' and use them to make a beach booklet which the children can illustrate.
✧ Look at the beach postcards and *Where's Wally?* book again, and play What can I? from looking at the pictures.
✧ Paint some beach pictures using a small amount of sand mixed with paint to give a textured effect.

DESERTS

Objective

Geography – to find out what life is like in hot, sandy deserts.

Group size

Up to five children.

What you need

A sand tray, dry sand, a collection of model camels and play people, a large cotton handkerchief, four strong twigs, red Cellophane paper, a shallow dish of water, tin foil, brown and green art paper, plastic bottles, scissors, Blu-Tack, some pictures of traditional desert head-dresses (keffiyehs) and clothing.

What to do

Set up the sand try ready for use with dry sand in it and let the children play in small groups to create a desert scene. Encourage them to create a journey through the desert, using the play people and model camels. They could even 'make camp' round an 'oasis', setting up a tent with twigs and a handkerchief, and red Cellophane for a fire. Show them how to make palm trees from paper and water bottles and miniature utensils from tin foil.

Discussion

Talk about how some parts of the world are called deserts and how some of these are very hot indeed, with dry sand, hardly any rain and often very cold nights. Ask the children to imagine an enormous beach with no houses, buildings, shops, or roads – just sand. Tell the children about the people who live in the deserts such as the nomadic Arabs who live in the Sinai desert and who travel with their 'caravans' of camels, setting up tents at night. Explain how the camels carry water and belongings and how they store food in their humps and water in their stomachs. Tell the children how the wind blows the sand into sand dunes (which the children could make in the sand tray with their fingers). Tell them about the hazards of sandstorms.

Follow-up activities

✧ Point out the desert regions (the Sahara in Africa, the Gobi in China and the Colorado in America) on a large world map or globe.
✧ Make a desert picture by painting a thin strip of blue across the top of some paper, for the sky, and then spreading glue over the rest of the paper. Show the children how to trickle dry sand across the paper through a paper funnel.
✧ Have a look at some cactus plants.
✧ Talk about desert animals, such as the fennel fox and the gerbil which burrow underground to escape the heat. If possible, bring in a gerbil and talk about the fur on the pads of its feet which prevent it from sinking into the sand.

SHADOW DANCE

Objective

PE – to explore body movements using shadows.

Group size

Up to six children.

What you need

A sunny day, an outside play area, chalk, a battery-operated cassette player, a cassette tape of children's lively dance music.

Preparation

Outside, chalk some oval shapes (approximately the size of a child's head), well spaced on a paved area.

What to do

Take the children outside and tell them that you are going to play them some music which they can dance to. Point out the oval shapes which you have chalked on the ground. Explain to them that when the music stops each child must try to position him / herself in such a way that the shadow of their head covers one of the oval shapes.

Play the music to them and let them dance around using all of their bodies in big expressive movements. Stop the music from time to time and check to see if they have managed to cover their 'shadow' heads with an oval.

Discussion

Talk about how, on sunny days, we can see our shadows. Point out that when we move, so does our shadow, but that as we move around our shadow does not always look the same shape and size as we are. Talk about how, on hot days, we can feel cool by standing underneath something, or by standing in its shadow. Explain that this is because it shades us from the heat of the sun.

Follow-up activities

✧ Let the children explore how they can move around in the sun and stand to make the shadows of their heads appear bigger and then smaller.
✧ Using a torch or table lamp (with shade removed) as the 'sun', let the children experiment with simple shadow puppets indoors. Use card shapes mounted on lolly sticks for the puppets. Fix up a large sheet of white paper to make shadows against.
✧ If it's a cloudy day and the children can't make shadows sing 'Sunshine calypso' on page 84 in an attempt to make the sun shine!

FADE OUT

Objective

Science - to find out about the sun's rays and its effects on certain materials.

Group size

Whole group.

What you need

Some sunny weather, white kitchen paper, scissors, Blu-Tack, adhesive tape, coloured sugar paper, a display board facing a sunny window, greetings cards and catalogues.

Preparation

Practise cutting-out skills using a selection of old greetings cards and catalogues. Ask the children to try cutting-out in straight lines and in curvy and wavy lines. Mount sheets of coloured sugar paper on a display board in direct sun.

What to do

Let the children stand in the sunny room so that they can feel the sunshine on their arms and faces as it shines through the window.

Talk about how the sun feels on us and what causes it. Give the children a circle each of white kitchen paper folded into quarters (older children will be able to fold the paper themselves). Show the children how to snip little pieces out of the folded

circles ('v' shapes are the easiest) all the way round and then open out the circles to reveal a doily.

Let the children each fix their named doilies to the display board with Blu-Tack or folded adhesive tape. Leave the display for a few days, then ask them to remove carefully their doilies one at a time.

Discussion

Ask the children if they can see how the background paper has changed colour where the doilies were. Can they tell you why the doilies have left a pattern on the background coloured paper? Wait to see if anyone realises that what has happened is that where the sugar paper was not covered the sun has faded it. Prove this by holding a fresh sheet of the same coloured sugar paper next to the faded piece. Explain how the sun's rays have faded the colour in the sugar paper. Discuss how in hot countries people keep their curtains or shutters closed in the heat of the day to prevent carpets and curtains becoming faded.

Follow-up activities

✧ Experiment by using different coloured sugar paper as the backing paper. What happens when white sugar paper is used?
✧ Ask the children to make up a 'fade out' picture. Let them draw and cut-out simple house, tree and flower shapes and stick them on to the sugar paper backing. Remove the shapes after a few sunny days to reveal a picture!

SUNFLOWERS

Objective

Art — to make finger paintings of sunflowers.

Group size

Up to four children.

What you need

Sunflowers (preferably real), magnifying glasses, a copy of the painting *Sunflowers* by Van Gogh, yellow, brown and green ready-mixed or powder paints, PVA adhesive, three plastic plates, paper, tissues (for wiping fingers), *The Tiny Seed* by Eric Carle (Hamish Hamilton).

Preparation

Add a little PVA adhesive to the paints and mix to a thick, creamy consistency. Put one colour on each of the plates.

What to do

Let the children carefully examine the real sunflowers, using a magnifying glass. Encourage them to gently stroke the petals and feel the seeds with their fingertips. Now show the children the picture of Van Gogh's *Sunflowers*.

When the children are familiar with the properties of the sunflowers let them paint their own versions, using their fingers. Provide the three plates with the ready-mixed paint and adhesive and let them create their own versions.

Discussion

Ask the children why they think sunflowers have this name. Show them the pages in *The Tiny Seed* which shows the sun next to a giant sunflower, and ask the children to tell you how a sunflower is like the sun (round, yellow, a sunny colour, bright, light, warm). Ask the children at what time of the year sunflowers (and other flowers) grow, and what they need to make them grow. Talk about the petals and the seeds, the stem and the leaves.

Follow-up activities

✧ Use paintbrushes, with possibly a potato masher, to print the effect of the seeds on to the sunflower finger paintings.
✧ Read *The Tiny Seed* and show the children the picture of the giant sunflower which grows taller than a house.
✧ Using lengths of wallpaper and small decorators' brushes, let the children paint sunflowers as big as themselves, with their own smiling 'sunny' face in the middle. When they are dry, mount the cut-out pictures to make 'Our garden of sunny smiles'.
✧ Let the children plant their own sunflower seeds and watch them grow.

FLY AWAY FLY!

Objective

Science – to perform a role-play to show how food must be protected from flies.

Group size

Three children at a time, while the rest of group watch and wait for their turn.

What you need

Cardboard box, white paper, scissors, adhesive or adhesive tape, empty milk carton, tub of margarine, pack of biscuits, biscuit tin, a sandwich, a plastic sandwich box, loaf of bread, bread bin, child's black leotard or black jumper, two tables.

Preparation

Help the children to turn the cardboard box into a refrigerator, by cutting out a 'hinged' door and covering the box with white paper. Turn one child into a 'fly' by dressing him/her in a black leotard or black jumper.

What to do

Pretend your area is a kitchen and place the milk carton, the margarine, the biscuits, the sandwich and the bread on a table in the centre. Arrange the 'refrigerator', the biscuit tin, the sandwich box and the bread bin on another table. Position two children in the 'kitchen' and the 'fly' (dressed in black), in the far corner of the room.

When you say 'Here comes the fly' the 'fly' must start to 'buzz' and 'fly' towards the kitchen. Tell the two children to quickly try to put all the food away into its correct containers before the 'fly' lands and reaches it!

Discussion

Talk about how, on hot days, we see many flies which carry germs. Explain how, if food is not put away properly, flies may touch the food, and leave their germs on it and how, if we eat that food, the germs might make us poorly.

Follow-up activities

✧ Explain how we use silver foil and protective film to keep food fresh. Let the children use some to wrap up real or replica food.
✧ Talk about how many foods will develop their own germs (bacteria) if they are not kept cool in a refrigerator, especially in hot weather. Demonstrate how margarine melts when left out, and how milk goes 'off'.

CHAPTER 2 RAIN

In this chapter children learn about rain at home and far away in the rain forest, through music, art and drama activities. They find out how to measure rainfall, as well as what to wear in wet weather.

INCY WINCY'S PUDDLE

Objective

Science – to find out about the rain cycle.

Group size

Up to six.

What you need

A small plastic spider, length of black wool, a kitchen roll tube, an empty water tray, yellow  and blue card, black felt-tipped pen, drinking straws (preferably transparent), adhesive tape, a jug, water, a copy of the rhyme 'Incey Wincey' from page 67.

Preparation

Attach the spider to the length of wool, and then tie the wool so that it is long enough for the spider to be pulled up and down the kitchen roll tube. Cut out a rectangle of blue card (approximately 16cm by 10cm). Cut out a yellow sun, and stick this at the top of the blue 'sky' card. Attach the straw to the back of the card, with adhesive tape, with approximately 1cm of straw protruding above the card, and 2cm below the card.

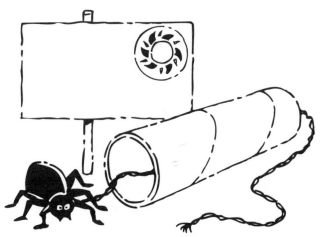

What to do

Recite the rhyme with the children and demonstrate how the spider climbs up the 'spout' (tube). Pour a small quantity of water down the tube, to 'wash the spider out'. Produce the 'sun', and show how the sun dries up the rain, by sucking up the 'puddle' through the straw. Providing a fresh straw each time, let each child make the spider go up and down the 'spout', and 'dry up' the rain, while the rest of the group recite the rhyme.

Discussion

Talk about drain pipes and how spiders can climb up bath and basin pipes. Ask what happens to puddles when the sun comes out, and talk about how the sun 'dries up' the water in puddles. Explain that when the tiny drops of water (which we cannot see) go up into the sky (evaporate), they meet lots of other tiny drops, and they join together to make big raindrops, which we can see. These big raindrops fall down from the sky and the process starts again.

Follow-up activities

✧ After some summer rain, let the children draw round puddles with chalk. Later on, they can see what has happened to the size of the puddles. Explain that some of the water has been 'dried up' by the sun (evaporated), but that some has gone into the ground.
✧ Sing the song 'When the blue skies turn to grey' page 86 and talk about the changing sky colour, during Incy's adventures.

HOW MUCH RAIN?

Objective

Mathematics – to measure rainfall in a home-made rain gauge.

Group size

Whole group, with pairs measuring and recording on a daily basis.

What you need

An empty washing-up liquid bottle, sharp scissors, an old tape measure, adhesive tape, two bricks.

Preparation

Draw a line round the bottle, about two thirds up from the bottom. Cut round the line and remove the nozzle. Turn the top section of the bottle upside down, and place firmly into the bottom section like a funnel. Cut the first ten centimetres off an old measuring tape and attach vertically to the rain gauge with adhesive tape. Find a suitable place outside, to place the rain gauge, and secure with bricks.

What to do

Explain to the children that you are going to keep a record of how much rain falls. Show them the measuring equipment and point out how to make a reading of any rain that has fallen.

Each day let the children go out in pairs with a helper to inspect the rain gauge and work out how many millimetres of rain have fallen. Encourage them to tell the rest of the group the result when they return. Keep a simple graph to show the rainfall measured. Note: It is best to measure and empty the rain guage at the same time of day.

Discussion

Talk about how we need rain to provide water which we keep in reservoirs ready to use. Talk about how important it is for us to know how much rain has fallen, and how much water there is in the reservoirs. Mention the effects of droughts, and floods. Show the rain gauge, and the tape measure down the side which shows how many millimetres or centimetres of rain have fallen. Explain to the children that if only a tiny amount of rain falls, which it is difficult to measure, then this is called a trace.

Follow-up activities

✧ Ask each child to bring in an empty washing-up liquid bottle to each make a rain gauge. During short breaks such as half-term let the children take home their gauges and make a rainfall record. They can bring their rain diary into the group afterwards.
✧ Make a large block graph to show the results.
✧ On a map of the world point out the countries with high and low rainfalls (rain forests / deserts).
✧ Find pictures of floods and droughts, display them with explanations written by the children.

PITTER PATTER PICTURES

Objective

Art – to use rain to help create 'drippy' pictures.

Group size

Up to eight.

What you need

Thin white card (old greetings cards), red, yellow and blue powder paints, newspaper, brushes, raincoats for children and adult, a rainy day, the song 'Storm Song' on page 69.

Preparation

Mix the powder paints to a fairly thin, runny consistency. Place your working table near an outside door, and cover it with newspaper. All put on your raincoats.

What to do

On a rainy day, look out of the window with the children and observe the journey of the raindrops down the window panes. Anticipate which drops will reach the bottom first. Encourage the children to listen for the 'pitter patter' sound of the rain falling and let them use their finger tips on the table to copy the sound. Sing the 'Storm Song', page 69.

Set up the table ready for your artwork and hand the children some card each to work on. Show them how to hold their brushes about 30cm above their head and recreate the raindrop effect by dropping paint on to their cards. Let the children then quickly take their cards outside into the rain and tilt them so that the paint drips, together with the raindrops, down to the bottom of the cards. Carefully return the cards to the horizontal position, and take them back inside to dry.

Discussion

Ask the children why they think the drips run down the window (and their cards) and not across or upwards. Talk about how the colours of the paints blend and change to make new colours, so that red and yellow make orange, and blue and yellow make green.

Follow-up activities

✧ Use dry brushes to sprinkle several colours of dry powder paint onto a card. Take the card outside in the rain, 'catch' some raindrops on the cards, quickly bring the card inside and see some 'pitter patter' raindrops.
✧ Make drip pictures indoors by blowing paint through drinking straws.
✧ Paint some card with a thin wash of icing sugar and water. Draw 'rain', using water-based felt-tipped pens, to create a very fuzzy, indistinct effect. Add someone walking with an umbrella.

KEEP DRY

Objective

Science – to find out that some materials are waterproof.

Group size

Up to six.

What you need

A large water tray, six dolls (preferably with hair), a selection of materials (cotton, velvet, plastic, wool, polyester, leather), dolls' party clothes, watering can, water, waterproof aprons, six safety pins.

Preparation

Cut the materials into six rain capes for the dolls, large enough to completely cover the clothes underneath. Tell the children to put on their aprons.

What to do

Give each child a doll to dress in party clothes and then tell them to put on one of the special rain capes over the top. Help them with the safety pin fastenings and ask them if they can name the material. Ask the children which of the rain capes they think will be most effective in keeping the dolls dry and why.

Taking turns, let the children each put their doll in the water tray and take turns to 'shower' it with 'rain' from the watering can. Lift the dolls out onto a large table and remove the rain capes, being careful to leave each cape next to its owner doll. Can the children see which doll has stayed the driest? Which doll is the wettest? Invite the children to put the capes in order from the most effective to the least effective.

Discussion

Ask the children which material they would choose for a raincoat and then compare their actual coats (check the labels to see what they are made of). Are some coats effective in light showers but not heavy rain? The dolls all have wet hair – how could this have been avoided? What should they have been wearing on their feet? What prevented the children getting wet while joining in the activity? (their waterproof aprons).

Follow-up activities

✧ Take the children for a walk in the rain wearing totally waterproof clothing including wellingtons for splashing in puddles!
✧ Experiment with using different materials to make umbrellas for the dolls.
✧ Sing the song 'Splish Splash' (page 81).
✧ Make a 'waterproof' chart showing materials in order of theireffectiveness against rain.

STORMS!

Objective

Music – to create storm sounds using percussion instruments.

Group size

Up to fifteen.

What you need

Percussion instruments (shakers, drums, bells, chime bars, tambourines, triangles, cymbals), chains, pictures of stormy weather, sugar paper, a thick magazine, taped bird song, the song 'Storm Song' from page 69.

Preparation

Cut out some storm cloud shapes (with zigzagged lightning if preferred) from the sugar paper.

What to do

Sing 'Storm Song' with the children. Make up a simple storm story together, taking time to use lots of onomatopoeic words such as 'splash, drip, bang, pitter, patter, crash'. Explain how a storm might start very slowly and quietly with just a few drops of rain and gradually build up to a crescendo with loud claps of thunder and flashes of lightning dying down. Show the children the pictures of stormy weather and discuss which of the percussion instruments could best represent light rain, heavy rain and thunder. (A thick magazine held at the spine and shaken, makes a good thunder sound).

If possible, darken the room to add to the atmosphere; pin up some of the sugar paper 'storm clouds' at the window. Watch out for any sensitive children who may be alarmed by the darkness and the noise and keep them close by.

Let the children each choose an instrument and they can then contribute appropriate 'sound effects' as you tell the story. As the 'thunder' dies down play some taped bird song, to show that the storm is over, and that nature returns to normal.

Discussion

Encourage the children to relate their own experiences of being in a storm. Were they frightened? Talk about the different kinds of storms such as tornadoes, hurricanes, sandstorms and snowstorms. Which instrument would best recreate these storms?

Follow up activities

✧ Introduce movement and dance to accompany the percussion.
✧ Let the children make up their own storm stories, and working in groups of three or four they can use the percussion instruments to put on a performance with one child as the narrator.

A BRAVE BOY

Objective

History — to find out about a historical story of bravery in a storm.

Group size

Whole group.

What you need

The story 'A brave boy' from page 80, sand tray, water, a green plastic play cloth, model houses, farm animals, hedges, fences, a blue plastic play cloth, a large baking tin, blue food colouring, a storage tray, a pencil, a watering can, pictures of dykes and seawalls.

What to do

Read the story to the children and tell them that they are going to act it out in the sand tray.

Working with the children, place the green play cloth over one half of the bottom of the tray, to represent the land. Arrange the play houses, hedges, fences and farm animals on top of the green play cloth. In the other half of the sand tray recreate the sea, by placing an upturned storage tray in the bottom and then covering it with the blue play cloth, so that the 'sea' is higher than the land.

Half fill the baking tin with water, to which a few drops of blue food colouring have been added. Place the baking tin on top of the blue play cloth. Let the children fashion a 'dyke' from sand and water, to separate the 'sea' from the 'land'. Use a pencil, to make a 'crack' in the dyke. Position a play person 'Peter' behind the 'crack'. Let the children blow on the sea, to recreate a 'storm', and let them take turns to make the 'rain' fall from the watering can near to the 'crack'.

Discussion

Explain the meaning of the word 'dyke' and 'leak'. Ask the children to tell you about any experiences they may have had at home of water leaking (bath overflowing and leaking into room downstairs, roof leaking, paddling pool). Ask why we cannot leave these leaks, and what we can do to stop them. What would happen if we did not repair them?

Follow-up activities.

◇ Let the children act out the story using props and costumes.
◇ Talk about what happens to our gardens, roads, rivers and football pitches when there is too much rain. Can the children think of any solutions?

HIGH OR LOW?

Objective

Mathematics – to sort animals according to their habitat positions in the rain forest.

Group size

Up to six children.

What you need

A climbing frame (with platform), sugar paper in various colours, scissors, old brown tights, sticky tape, green and brown curtains, soft toys and/or model animals (rhinoceros, deer, monkeys, squirrels, birds) as reference, thick string, large world map, cassette tape of animal music (such as the *Carnival of the animals* by Saint Saens), felt-tipped pens.

Discussion

Tell the children that in the rain forest it rains nearly every day, and it is very hot too. Use the world map to point out some rain forests (South America, Africa and Malaysia.) Talk about how all the trees and plants grow very quickly because of the rain and sunshine, and how the leaves of all the trees are very close together so that it looks as if there is a 'roof' of leaves, or 'canopy'. Explain that some animals live high up on top of this canopy, and that some animals live underneath the canopy low down in the undergrowth. In the Malaysian rain forest for example, gibbons, orang-utans, flying lizards, flying squirrels and birds live in the canopy and leopards, rhinoceroses, tapirs, butterflies, frogs and snakes live underneath the canopy.

What to do

Use the 'Discussion' section first to inform the children about rain forests. Following this discussion use a climbing frame as the basis for a rain forest. Place some brown curtaining under the frame for the 'undergrowth' and cover the platform with green material for the 'canopy' of leaves at the tops of the trees. Let the children wrap old, brown tights round the posts of the frame, to represent tree trunks.

Draw large leaf shapes on green sugar paper and cut them out. These can then be stuck around the frame using sticky tape. Let the children choose which animal they want to be and make simple masks to represent them.

Play the music and tell the children to dance around the frame adopting the movements of their chosen animals. When the music stops and you say 'night-time', the children have to find the appropriate place in the 'rain forest' either high up above the canopy of the leaves (on the platform), or below it, in the 'undergrowth' to go to sleep.

Follow-up activities

✧ Unroll a length of wallpaper and paint rain forest trees on the back. Draw or paint some animals on another section of paper, cut them out, and stick them among the trees, either 'high up' or 'low down'.

✧ Talk about the destruction of the rain forests, and what we can do to avoid using too much wood and paper.

RAINBOW RHYME

Objective

Music – to experience and express a rhyme with a rhythmic beat.

Group size

Whole group.

What you need

A copy of the rhyme 'Rainbow rhyme' on page 73, two large pieces of white paper, black felt-tipped pen, crayons, percussion instruments, hard-backed books (one for each child).

Preparation

Copy out the rhyme on to one of the pieces of paper, underlining the 'colour' words in the appropriate colour. Display the paper where all the children can see it. On the other piece of paper draw a rainbow to illustrate the order of the colours and display this next to the rhyme.

What to do

Read the rhyme out loud to the children using a deliberate rap-like rhythm, and pointing to the words as you speak. Repeat the rhyme through several times and encourage the children to join in.

Next, recite the rhyme and let the children join in by clapping or tapping on the cover of a hard-backed book on their laps. Now, recite the rhyme using percussion instruments.

After this, let the children try clapping and tapping out the rhyme without saying the words Finally ask them to use the instruments alone without the words.

Discussion

Talk about how it is very important for everyone to clap, tap or play together, 'at the same time', to feel the rhythm of a rhyme or song properly. Talk about how the drummers in a marching band or pop group help everyone to 'keep time' and march and play together. Ask the children to pretend they are drummers when they are tapping or 'drumming' on the backs of their books.

Follow-up activities

✧ Use crêpe paper to make seven sashes, one for each colour of the rainbow. Choose seven children to each wear a sash – invite them to sit in a row at the front of the group and each choose an instrument to play. As the rest of the group recite the rhyme, the child wearing the appropriate coloured sash stands up and plays his/her instrument at the sound of his/her colour.

✧ Make a sash for every child and divide the children into seven groups; each group wearing a sash to represent a different colour of the rainbow. Let each child choose an instrument. Recite the rhyme out loud and at the mention of each colour, the 'matching' group stands up and plays.

CHAPTER 3
WIND

Activities in this chapter show children how to design kites, weather vanes, windmills and wind chimes. They also have the chance to sail boats on a windy day.

WINDY DAYS

Objective

English – to use descriptive language about the effects of the wind.

Group size

Up to ten children.

What you need

Balloons, string, a washing line, two men's shirts, two pillow cases, pegs.

Preparation

An adult should blow up the balloons, knot them and tie a length of string to each one. Talk with the children about the noise made if a balloon pops and explain that they should not be frightened if this happens. Set up a washing line outside. Rinse the shirts and pillow cases, squeeze them out and peg them on the washing line.

What to do

On a windy day take the children outside to observe the effects of the wind on the trees, leaves, grass, flowers, litter and the clothes you have pegged on the washing line. Ask the children to notice all the movement and to think of words to describe what they can see. Tell them to think about what they can see but also what they can hear and smell.

Encourage the children to move freely in the wind, walking, running and jumping in all directions, and spinning around. As they move ask them to describe how they feel (dizzy, cold, pushed about, buffeted).

Lastly, give each child a balloon on a string, and ask them to move as they did before, but tell them to hold on tightly to their balloons and not to let go. Ask them to talk about what they feel the wind is 'doing' to them as they try to hold on to their balloons.

Discussion

Ask: can we see the wind? How do we know it's there? Can you see anything bending, fluttering or billowing? Can you hear any rustling? What other sounds can you hear? How do your cheeks, eyes and fingers feel? Can you feel the wind tugging on your balloon? What else is it trying to do?

Follow-up activities

✧ Create group 'windy poems' by writing down the children's phrases, in a 'list' form which the children could illustrate.
✧ Say the poem 'The shirts on the line' on page 68, and copy the postures for each weather type.
✧ With older children talk about the Beaufort scale which measures wind force. See *Weather facts* (Pockets Full of Knowledge series, Dorling Kindersley). Draw pictures to illustrate the different forces of the wind.

WIND AND WAVES

Objective

Science — to observe the effects of the wind on water and home-made sailing boats.

Group size

Up to four children.

What you need

A washing-up bowl, a water tray, jugs, small polystyrene food trays, toothpicks, paper, crayons or felt-tipped pens, Blu-Tack. Pictures of sailing boats, a calm sea and a stormy sea.

Preparation

Fill the washing-up bowl with water. Take the water tray outside, on a windy day, and fill it almost to overflowing, so that the wind will 'catch' it, and blow it into ripples and small 'waves'.

What to do

Make simple sailing boats with the children, using polystyrene trays with cut-out paper sails attached to toothpicks and stuck into the 'boats' using a small blob of Blu-Tack. Try out the boats inside in the washing-up bowl, and then outside in the water tray. What differences can they see between 'sailing' their boats indoors and outside in the wind?

Discussion

Talk about a calm sea and a 'choppy' or 'stormy' sea, full of waves. Show the children the pictures you have available. Ask them if they know what makes the waves. Why don't the boats in the washing up bowl move unless they are pushed? What makes them move in the water tray outside? Ask what sailing boats do when the wind 'dies down' and the sea is becalmed. How do the boats move then? Ask whether sailing boats always have to move in the direction that the wind is blowing. What must boats do, if they want to sail in another direction?

Follow-up activities

✧ Make model 'wind surfers', by cutting out a polystyrene 'surf board' and attaching a toothpick 'sail', and a play figure, using adhesive tape.
✧ Paint pictures of sailing boats on a windy day using straws to blow 'the sea'.
✧ Say the rhyme 'The sail song' on page 70.

A BRAVE GIRL

Objective

History – to re-enact a true story of heroism on a windswept, stormy sea.

Group size

Whole group as the audience, five children acting out the story.

What you need

Two tables, two old, long curtains (preferably dark and plain), adhesive parcel tape, four long kitchen foil tubes, two empty cereal packets, scissors, dressing-up clothes (including two nightdresses and a shawl), three cushions, three blankets, pictures of lighthouses, the story 'A brave girl' on page 79.

Preparation

Make a 'rock' by covering one table with a curtain. Transform the second table into a rowing boat by turning it upside down, winding the curtain around the legs and securing it with parcel tape (don't make it too deep). Wrap protective cloth around the leg ends if necessary. Make two sets of 'oars' by cutting out four paddle shapes from cereal packets. Make two slits at the bottom of each tube, and insert the 'paddles'. Arrange the 'rock' table to one side of the 'stage' area, and the 'lighthouse', represented by three 'beds' (cushions and blankets) on the other side. The 'boat' should be between the 'rock' and the 'lighthouse', (in the 'sea'), so that it can be climbed into and out of from both the 'lighthouse' and the 'rock'.

What to do

Select five children to act out the story and take them aside. Tell the story on page 79 to these children only. One child will act as Grace, two her parents and two children the survivors. Repeat the story slowly, with pauses, helping the children to mime the appropriate actions. Older children may like to add a few words of dialogue.

When the 'actors' know what to do, assemble the other children together as an audience. Introduce the play by talking about the points in 'Discussion' below. Re-read the story aloud as the children act it out. Encourage the audience to provide the sound effects of the raging sea.

Discussion

Explain the importance of lighthouses, and how families used to live in them. Talk about how strong winds can blow the sea into a storm with high waves, and how in storms ships can run aground. Talk about how today lighthouses are automatic.

Follow-up activities

✧ Make a table model, using a cardboard tube for the lighthouse, crumpled newspaper covered in blue tissue paper for the sea, a cardboard boat and play people.
✧ Tell the children about the work of the lifeboat and air/sea rescue teams today.
✧ Read *The Lighthouse Keeper's Catastrophe* by Ronda and David Armitage (Picture Puffin).

FLYING HIGH!

Objective

Design and technology – to make a simple kite.

Group size

Up to four children.

What you need

Tissue paper, three polythene carrier bags, cardboard carton, heavy wallpaper (anaglypta), scissors, strong nylon wool, string, shears, a sharp knife, adhesive tape, parcel tape. Small, coloured sticky labels, eight garden canes, tracing paper, felt-tipped pens, examples of real kites (if possible) or pictures.

Preparation

Cut out four squares, each measuring 15cm by 15cm, one of tissue paper, one of polythene (cut from a carrier bag), one of cardboard (use a carton) and one of heavy wallpaper.

Cut open the other two carrier bags, each one into two pieces (ready for use later). Lay two of the garden canes on top of one of the polythene pieces in a cross shape. Secure the canes together with sticky tape and wool. Cut the canes to appropriate lengths, ensuring that the horizontal one is shorter than the vertical one. Carefully make a slit in the end of each garden cane and thread the wool around the outside to make a 'skeleton' of a diamond kite. Make sufficient 'skeleton' kites for each child to have one. (Before you begin, make sure that the children behave safely with the polythene and ensure that they are not left unattended while you are using it.)

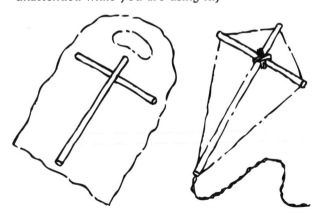

What to do

Tell the children they are going to each make a kite, but firstly they need to decide on the best material to use. 'Test' the squares of tissue paper, polythene, cardboard and heavy wallpaper, both inside and outside, to see which material flies the highest. Polythene should prove the most effective material.

Back inside, let the children examine the real kites and look at the pictures, and assist them to make a kite each. Each child should place the 'skeleton' on top of their piece of polythene and then fold the polythene over, securing it with parcel tape. Invite older children to work in pairs.

Encourage the children to draw their own designs on tracing paper with felt-tipped pens and to stick the designs on the front of their kites using adhesive tape. Add a piece of wool, 35cm long, as a tail, and decorate this by folding and sticking coloured sticky labels at intervals along the length of the wool. Stick on the tail with parcel tape, and add a 'flying cord' made of string.

Go back outside and fly the kites one at a time to start off with.

Discussion

Which square flew the highest, and the lowest? Why? Which material would tear most easily? Which would be the strongest? What would happen in the rain?

Follow-up activities

✧ Tell the children about the Chinese kite festival 'Climbing the heights', which occurs in September. Spectacular kites made to look like people, birds, butterflies and dragons are flown.
✧ Make a simple kite from a small polystyrene fruit tray. Trim off the curved edges and add a flying cord and tail. Use a thick marker pen to draw a pattern on the 'kite'.

WINDY PICTURES

Objective

Art — to create collage pictures of windy days.

Group size

Up to six children.

What you need

A variety of collage materials, both manufactured and natural (leaves, twigs, pieces of material, string, paper, tiny pebbles, corrugated card), dry sponges, dry grey, white and black powder paint on saucers. Photographs of windy days showing breezes, gales and hurricanes.

Preparation

If possible go for a walk on a very windy day or alternatively look at the windy day pictures. Talk about how people have to bend their bodies and bow their heads in the wind, how their clothes move, how umbrellas are blown inside out, how trees sway, and kites soar in the sky. Show pictures of seas in a hurricane, and discuss the colour of the sky. Let the children talk about any personal experiences they have had on windy days, and let them decide what sort of windy day picture they would like to create. Prepare the tables and put out all the collage materials for the children to select from.

What to do

As the children assemble their chosen collage pictures, help them to place the items so that they appear to be blowing in one direction. When the pictures are complete, add the effect of wind blowing by sponging on a small amount of dry powder paint in a swirling motion directly onto the paper. Use paint in various shades of grey, made by mixing the grey, white and black paint.

Discussion

Are the people on your picture able to walk in the wind or do they have to wait until the wind dies down? If you have ever been out in a very strong wind, did you have to close your eyes for a moment? Why? Have you ever had anything blown in your face, or round your legs?

Follow-up activities

✧ Make pictures of forests in the wind by painting the tree trunks, letting them dry, and then painting branches in a watery brown paint blown with a straw to create the effect of the wind.
✧ Sing the song 'Blow wind blow' on page 85.
✧ Talk about, and, if possible, show pictures of various winds around the world such as the desert whirlwinds of the Sahara in North Africa, the rain-bearing monsoons of Southern Asia and Africa, and the tornadoes, the rotating, stormy winds of America, which can lift cars and trees into the air. Let the children make pictures of these.

ACTIVITIES

WHICH WAY?

Objective

Design and technology – to make a wind vane and to learn the points of the compass.

Group size

Up to four children.

What you need

Card, scissors, adhesive tape, felt-tipped pens, four pen tops, four thin garden canes or pencils, damp sand, four plastic play buckets, a table, four small compasses, four chairs.

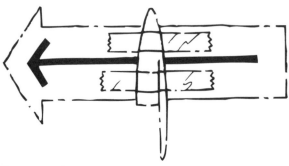

Preparation

Cut out four card pieces approximately 7cm by 2cm and draw an arrow on each one with a felt-tipped pen, on both sides of the card. Stick each card arrow on to a pen top with adhesive tape. Talk about how winds do not blow the same way, but come from different directions, which are called north, south, east, or west. Show the children a compass and explain how this can help us to find out which direction the wind is blowing from.

What to do

Let each child fill a play bucket with damp sand and stick a thin garden cane in the middle. Give each child the pen top with the arrow attached and ask each child to place it on top of their cane. Go outside and let each child place his/her 'wind vane' on a chair. Give each child a compass.

Let each child discover, and point to, north, south, east, and west, and collectively decide on one 'landmark' (a tree, building or a gate for example) to represent each direction. Now ask each children to observe to which 'landmark' his/her arrow is pointing. Let the children use their compasses to verify whether their arrow is pointing north, south, east or west. (Explain that if their arrow is pointing northwards, then a north wind is blowing – a wind vane points to where the wind is coming from). Let the children check each others vanes, to see they are all pointing the same way.

Ask the children to move their own chairs to different positions, and to check that their vanes still point in the original direction. Leave the vanes for a time, and see if they have changed direction.

Discussion

Which landmark is your vane pointing to? Is that north, south, east or west? How do you know? Can you see anything else that is being blown in that direction? (Litter or leaves.)

Follow-up activities

✧ Let the children record wind directions during the course of the day or over a week.
✧ Read *The Wind Blew* by Pat Hutchins (Red Fox) to the children.
✧ Play the 'Don't get lost!' game (photocopiable page 90) – four friends have been building snowmen in the park. Now there is a snowstorm and each friend must get home quickly in the right direction. Put four counters in the park and throw a dice marked '1, 2, 0, 1, 2, 0' to see who gets home first.

WORKING WIND

Objective

Design and technology – to make a simple windmill.

Group size

Up to four children.

What you need

Paper, a ruler, pencil, scissors, crayons or felt-tipped pens, an awl, adhesive tape, drinking straws with flexible 'necks', two toy 'seaside' windmills.

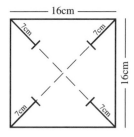 

Preparation

Cut the paper into squares 16cm by 16cm, fold each square into a triangle, and again into a further triangle. Fold it out flat and make pencil marks 7cm along each crease.

What to do

Let the children examine the two shop-bought windmills and carefully take one apart to show the children how it is constructed.

Help each child to cut along the diagonal creases on their paper square, as far as the pencil mark. Help each child to fold alternate corners of the paper into the centre, with a generous amount of 'overlap' of the four corners. Now push an awl through the four corners and the centre of the paper (an adult must do this). Remove the awl and insert a felt-tipped pen carefully through the hole. Gently twist the pen to enlarge the hole. Remove the pen and insert a straw through the

hole. Keep enlarging the size of the hole, with the felt-tipped pen, if necessary, until the mill spins freely on the straw when blown. The short section of the straw above the 'neck' should protrude through the front of the mill. Wind a small piece of adhesive tape at the front, short end of the straw to stop the mill coming off the end of the straw.

Let the children take their windmills outside, to experiment with standing still, walking and running with them, in different directions.

Discussion

Ask the children when their windmills turned most quickly, and when they turned slowly or not at all. Can the children explain why?

Follow-up activities

✧ Show the children pictures of windmills, and talk about how they were used for grinding grain, sawing up wood, pumping water on to dry land and to feed cattle. Today, in countries, such as Holland they are also used for pumping water away from very 'marshy' land. Special windmills are used in windy places to generate electricity.

✧ Read the poem 'Wind farm' on page 71.

✧ Make a drawing of a windmill and attach moving sails to it, made from two rectangular pieces of card secured with a split pin, loosely bent.

TINKLE, TINKLE

Objective

Music – to make indoor wind chimes.

Group size

Up to five children.

What you need

Small plastic 'hoopla' hoops, string, rings, bunches of old keys, seashells, small metal percussion instruments (such as bells, wire coat hangers, tin cans, cutlery).

Preparation

Talk about how the wind can blow objects together to make sounds and ask the children to think of some examples such as a door slamming shut, leaves rustling or tin cans rolling. Explain that many people around the world put together special objects to blow in the wind, because they like to hear the sound of these 'wind chimes'.

What to do

Ask the children to suggest small objects which the wind could blow together to make an indoor wind chime. Let the children assemble these and/ or bring some in from home. It is best to keep to small items such as keys, percussion bells, individual keys from a xylophone or shells.

Consider where the wind chimes should be hung to 'catch' some of the wind from outside (even a gentle breeze). When you have a collection of items, tie them individually on dangling string. Then tie them all on to a small 'hoopla' ring, and suspend this in your chosen place (near an open window or doorway – well above head height!).

Discussion

What is the best way to hang these (keys, bells, and so on) so that they 'bump' into one another and make a sound? How close together should they be, side by side, one in front of the other, two together, one on top of the other?

Follow-up activities

✧ Try making larger chimes to hang outdoors from trees or a sturdy bush.
✧ Ask the children: why are wind chimes useful in a house (to disturb flies), or a shop (to announce a customer), or outside (to frighten away birds from eating newly planted seeds)?

CHAPTER 4
CLOUDS AND FOG

In this chapter children will be able to see 'raindrops' being formed inside a 'cloud'. They will consider what can be done to reduce smog and, with Postman Pat, experience the problems caused by fog.

LIKE AN ICE-CREAM IN THE SKY

Objective
Art – to make cloud mobiles.

Group size
Up to six children.

What you need
White paper or card, straws, pencils, scissors, tracing paper, cotton wool, adhesive, wool (grey, or white flecked with silver or black), adhesive tape, silver glitter, invisible thread, pictures of clouds, white, grey and black powder paint, paintbrushes.

Preparation
Tie pairs of thin straws together in a cross shape, using adhesive tape. Prepare the children by drawing their attention to the clouds in the sky when they go outside to play or at home time. Ask the children what the different shapes remind them of They may suggest – a cauliflower, smoke, Father Christmas's beard, mountains and lakes, waves, animals, a giant ice-cream. Ask the children to describe the clouds (fluffy, blobby, ripply, bubbly, blotchy, patchy, wispy).

What to do
After the children have had the chance to observe a variety of cloud types in the sky, ask them to make some drawings of their favourites. Can they describe them to you?

Let them choose some cloud shapes to reproduce for a mobile. They can draw their cloud shapes on paper, card, or tracing paper and then cut them out and paint them. Help them to attach invisible thread to each one, before tying it to the ends of straws. Vary the cloud types using different paints and adding glitter to some. 'Rain clouds' for example can be made by painting in shades of grey and adding silver glitter. Stick short lengths of appropriately coloured wool to the bottom of the clouds (to look like rain) to finish.

Discussion
Are clouds the same colour all over? What colours and shades do you need to paint a rain cloud? What does a thundercloud look like?

Follow-up activities
✧ Make a three-dimensional 'cloudscape' by suspending the mobiles inside a large, rectangular carton, lined with blue paper.
✧ Talk about how aeroplanes leave vapour trails, or contrails made of ice crystals in their 'exhaust fumes'; suspend cardboard planes and trails made of cotton wool in the 'cloudscape' box.
✧ Talk about the phrases 'walking on air' and being on 'cloud nine'; have the children ever felt like this?
✧ Make up fantasy adventures about being blown by the wind up into 'cloudland'.

MAKE A CLOUD

Objective

Science – to demonstrate that clouds are made up of tiny water droplets.

Group size

Up to six children.

What you need

An electric kettle, lead, power point, table, large plastic bottle.

What to do

Make sure the children are sat well back from the table and warn them to stay seated. Turn the kettle on to boil and as soon as the steam appears, place the bottle over the spout to fill the bottle with steam. When the bottle is cloudy, replace the cap.

Let the children hold the bottle to the light and watch the 'cloudiness' turn into 'raindrops'. Explain that the water in the kettle is like water in a puddle, and that when the kettle gets hot some of the water turns into 'wet air' (evaporates), just as the sun makes some of the water in a puddle turn into 'wet air'. Tell the children that the sun makes this happen much more slowly than the electricity heating the kettle water.

Point out that we cannot actually see the sun evaporating puddle water, but that we can see it happening with the kettle, in the steam. Explain that the steam caught in the bottle is made from millions of tiny, invisible water droplets, and that the children can watch the steam turning back into 'raindrops', as the droplets join together and that this is just what happens in clouds.

Discussion

What is a cloud made of? Is the air in a cloud dry or 'wet'? Where do the water droplets in the 'wet air' come from? How do the water droplets get into the clouds? What happens to the water droplets inside a cloud?

Follow-up activities

✧ Talk about high, medium and low clouds, and how hail, snow, sleet and thunderclouds are often produced by high and medium clouds, while mist and fog are low clouds.
✧ Talk about a 'cloudburst' and thunderclouds, in which strong winds make the water droplets rub against each other, causing lightning. This makes hot air which pushes against cold air causing thunder. Create some powerful artwork to show thunder and lightning storms.
✧ Paint pictures of storms where strong winds blow spiders, maggots, or sticklebacks about.

FOGGY MORNINGS

Objective

Music – to represent 'foggy morning' sounds with percussion instruments.

Group size

Up to ten children, with rest of group as audience.

What you need

A plain net curtain, adhesive tape, thick string, rulers, card, scissors, felt-tipped pen, handbells, woodblock, guiro, sandblocks, tambourine, chime bars, two tables, two chairs.

Preparation

Help the children to cut out card 'stick puppets' to represent a milkman, a postlady, a cat, a fire-engine and a car; stick a ruler to the bottom of each figure to make a 'handle'. Suspend some string about four feet high, and hang the net 'fog' over the string, folded several times. Place one table behind the 'fog', and two chairs behind the table. Put the card puppets and instruments (see 'What you need') on a table behind the chairs.

What to do

Let the children take turns to sit two at a time on the chairs, behind the 'fog' net. One child can manoeuvre a card figure, while the other child provides the sound-effects. The children in the 'audience' have to work out what is happening. Suggestions for 'foggy morning scenarios' are:

Card puppet	Sound effect
The milkman arrives, falls over a stone, and breaks the bottles.	Tambourine
The postlady arrives on her bicycle.	Handbells
Mum or dad de-ice the car windscreen (foggy mornings are often icy, too).	Sandblocks
The car won't start.	Repeated strokes on a guiro
The cat gets lost and ends up stuck in a tree.	Handbells
The fire-engine is called.	Siren; two notes on the chime bars

Discussion

Fog and mist are clouds which are very low down in the sky. They can be so 'thick' that it is very difficult to see people, buildings and traffic. If we cannot see in fog and mist, how can we know what is happening? What must car drivers use on foggy days? (Head lights and fog lights.)

Follow-up activities

✧ While one child turns his/her back, another sits behind the 'fog' and speaks. Who is it?
✧ The children line up as 'fog bound' planes at the airport, covered in a net curtain. Only when the 'fog' is lifted can the planes take off.
✧ Add another table on the other side of the suspended net curtain, and position boats to make a 'fog bank' at sea. Making 'fog horn' sounds, the children can move the boats but they must try not to collide.
✧ Sing the song 'A Foggy Day' on page 86.

DOWN ON THE FOGGY FARM

Objective

PE – to move like farm animals.

Group size

Up to whole group (space permitting).

What you need

A collection of toy farm animals (one for each child), a drawstring bag, a torch, a 'farmer's hat', chime bars.

What to do

Select one child as the farmer who will wear the hat. Tell this child to turn his or her back, while you put a collection of toy farm animals into a drawstring bag (one for each child present). These can include cows, hens, sheep, pigs, goats, ducks, geese, dogs, cats and horses.

In turn the children can take a toy animal out of the bag, note what it is, and replace it in the bag,

remembering 'their' animal. Turn off the lights to recreate a dark foggy morning. Tell all the children to spread out 'in the fog', while the 'farmer' comes to search for a certain 'lost' animal. All the children move making appropriate movements for their animal without making a sound. The 'farmer' walks through the animals, looking to see who is moving like the 'lost' animal.

Play the chime bars slowly, perhaps just two notes repeated, as everyone moves around. When you stop playing, the 'farmer' says: 'I'm looking for my lost …', and shines the torch on one child s/he thinks might be the 'lost' animal. If correct, this 'animal' then moves appropriately towards the 'farmer', this time making the appropriate sounds. This child now becomes the 'farmer'.

Discussion

If a farmer 'loses' an animal in the fog, and cannot see it, what can s/he use to try and 'see through' the fog? How do animals move their bodies, especially their legs, tails or wings?

Follow-up activities

✧ Play 'sheep dogs' – one child 'rounds up' the 'sheep', to the left, and right, drives them gently round obstacles, puts them in a pen, and lets them out again.
✧ Look at some cowbells, and talk about how sheep and lambs are marked to identify them, in case they stray.

POSTMAN PAT'S FOGGY DAY

Objective

Mathematics — to practise sequencing skills and time vocabulary.

Group size

Whole group.

What you need

The story 'The foggy day' from page 74, paper, felt-tipped pens, scissors, five pegs, thick string.

Preparation

Cut the paper into five rectangles, each measuring 32cm by 44cm. On the first draw a picture of a crossroads sign, as seen in the fog; on the second draw the outline of a scarecrow; on the third a tractor in the fog; on the fourth sheet, draw Jess the cat on a 'tussock'; and on the fifth draw a church tower, with bells visible in the belfry. Suspend the string across a clear space and attach the pegs at intervals.

What to do

Read the story aloud to all the children. Once they are familiar with the story, read it again and at intervals ask individual children to select and hang up the correct pictures so that they are in the correct chronological order. As each child selects a picture encourage them to 'talk through' the events in the story, using the correct time vocabulary, for example: before, after, first, second, and next.

Discussion

After they have heard the story, ask the children: What was the first thing Postman Pat saw in the fog? What was the second? What did he see after that? What did Postman Pat hear in the end?

Follow-up activities

✧ Play 'foggy day' letters; hang numbered paper 'doors' on the string, each with a cut-out letter box, let a child stand behind each door. Address envelopes to different people in the 'street' and let one child, 'Pat', post the letters through the wrong doors, as he 'cannot see the numbers properly in the fog'. The children behind the doors must then deliver the letters correctly to their neighbours.
✧ Invite a guide, scout, ranger or climber in to talk about walking, camping or climbing safely in the countryside, and what to do if bad weather occurs, especially fog. Ask them to show the children a survival kit.

CAN YOU SEE IT?

Objective

Art – to recreate a foggy day scene using a wax-resist technique.

Group size

Up to eight children.

What you need

White paper, wax crayons, thinly mixed grey powder paint, paintbrushes.

What to do

Ask the children to draw a picture of an outdoors scene using wax crayons. When they are happy with their scene show them how to paint over their drawings with thinly mixed grey powder paint. Let them see what happens and ask: Can you still see your picture?

Discussion

Ask the children to think about foggy days and what certain objects might look like in the fog, such as the branches of a tree looking like a giant's fingers, lorries looking like dragons, people looking like ghosts and so on. Ask the children whether or not the 'fog' paint covers the wax crayon properly. Talk about how the water in the paint 'runs off' the crayon. Can the children think of anything else that makes water 'run off' it?

Follow-up activities

✧ Using black paper and watery black paint, let the children create 'Foggy night' pictures, using silver crayons for the moon and stars, and yellow crayons for illuminated windows and car headlamps.
✧ Read the poem 'Fog' on page 69. Paint a scene you might see through a window, cover it with a piece of tracing paper, to create a 'foggy' appearance. Cut out a piece of yellow paper as the 'sun' and let the children alternate foggy and sunny weather in their scene.
✧ Cut-out pictures of cars, houses, trees, people and animals from magazines and greetings cards. Assemble them on paper to create outdoor scenes, and then cover with tracing paper, to represent fog.

NOT TOO FAST!

Objective

PE – to use body movements to represent traffic in fog.

Group size

Up to eight children.

What you need

Cereal packets, scissors, play figures, play fruit, adhesive tape, a copy of the song 'A foggy day' on page 86, a play police hat.

adhesive tape to secure the figures.

Preparation

Cut open the cereal packets to provide the large rectangular sides of the packet for the children to use. Stick some play figures (up to four) on top of the packet sides, ideally they should be sitting as if they were in a car. Similarly, stick up to about ten figures on other packet sides, to represent people sitting on a bus. Stick some play fruit on other sides to represent fruit lorries travelling to a supermarket. Ask each child to adopt a crawling position, and stick a 'car', 'bus' or 'lorry' on to each child's back with adhesive tape.

What to do

Let the children sing or recite the words to the song 'A foggy day' and as they do so they can crawl around the floor very slowly, moving like traffic in fog. Remind the children to crawl slowly so that they do not 'crash' and endanger their passengers or merchandise. Choose one 'dangerous' driver who should forget to crawl, and move too quickly, and so attract the attention of the traffic police officer (you!).

Discussion

Why is it so important for traffic to move slowly in foggy weather? What will happen if vehicles travel too quickly? As you are driving in fog, what kind of things might you not see very clearly? (Pedestrians, traffic lights, road signs and so on.) What should vehicles do to try and make sure that other vehicles know they are there?

Follow-up activities

✧ Discuss with the children why people make traffic journeys in the morning, and what the consequences might be if the traffic has to slow down because of fog. Try to reassure the children that it never matters if people are late because of fog. For example, if a school bus is late arriving at school, then school simply opens later than usual. Stress that traffic must never hurry in fog, to make sure that there are no accidents on the road.
✧ Bring in reflective and luminous arm bands and clothing worn on dark, foggy mornings. Bring in a bicycle with its reflectors.
✧ Invite a 'lollipop' person, traffic police officer or representative of a motoring organisation to talk about road safety in foggy weather.

SMOG

. . . .

Objective

RE – to encourage an awareness of the environment.

Group size

Six children; remainder of group as audience.

What you need

Eighteen chairs, a child's tricycle, a cycle mask, a box of fruit, quoits, newspaper, scissors, adhesive tape, cardboard tubes, green paper, and a 'sit and ride' train.

Preparation

With the children, set up a 'traffic jam', consisting of four 'cars' (each made from four chairs – two in front, two behind), a child's tricycle and a 'lorry' (made from a chair, behind which is another chair on which sits a box of fruit) – all 'one behind the other'. Roll the newspaper into tubes, fringe the ends with scissors. Stick several of these tubes behind each car and the lorry, to represent 'exhaust fumes'.

What to do

Tell the children that they are going to pretend to be drivers stuck in a traffic jam in the smog. Position one child as the 'driver' in each of the 'cars', another child on the tricycle, wearing a cycle mask, and another child as the 'lorry driver'. Use a quoit as a 'steering wheel'. Tell the children to cough and look glum because they are stuck in a traffic jam in the 'smog'. They should talk to each other in the 'jam', about how traffic and fumes can be reduced. They can then transform the 'jam' accordingly (remove three of the cars, and the drivers all get into one car and remove the lorry and pretend to put the fruit on a train). This will leave only one car with four happy passengers and one happy cyclist who no longer needs a mask!

Discussion

'Smog' is a mixture of fog and smoke, which makes us cough. Where does the smoke come from? Is it a good idea to have lots of cars on the roads, with just one driver in each car? What could we do about this? Is it a good idea to have lots of lorries on the roads, all taking goods to shops and factories? In what other way could the goods travel?

Follow-up activities

✧ Let the children draw traffic pictures with grey wool stuck behind each vehicle, to represent exhaust fumes.

✧ Use a floor mat to set up a traffic jam using toy cars. Count how many people could fit in toy buses instead, and then take a corresponding number of cars 'off the road'.

✧ Use photocopiable page 91 to reinforce environmental awareness.

CHAPTER 5
SNOW AND ICE

In this chapter children have the opportunity to handle real snow and ice, they can pretend to be hibernating animals in the snow, as well as dancing snowmen. They even have the chance to recreate Scott's Antarctic expedition!

SNOWY POEMS

Objective

English – to describe sensory experiences of snow.

Group size

Up to six children.

What you need

Newly-fallen snow, a clipboard, paper, pen, five pieces of card (A4-sized), felt-tipped pens, sugar paper, stapler.

Preparation

Prepare a large book, with a sugar paper cover entitled 'Snow'. Provide five pages entitled: 'Snow looks ...'; 'Snow feels ...'; 'Snow sounds ...'; 'Snow smells ...'; and 'Snow tastes ...'. On the first card draw a large eye, on the second card, a pair of hands, on the third an ear, on the fourth, a nose, and a mouth on the fifth.

What to do

On a snowy day, make sure the children are dressed very warmly, and take them out into some newly-fallen snow.

To focus their attention on experiencing snow through each of the senses, in turn hold up the 'sense' cards. Ask the children to describe how snow looks, feels, sounds, smells and tastes and note down what the children say. Back inside, depending on the age of the group, you and/or the children can write and illustrate the observations which have been made, on the appropriate pages of the 'Snow book'. This should provide a blank verse poem on each page of the 'Snow book'.

Discussion

What does the snow look like to you? What things does it remind you of? How does the snow feel when you pat it, squeeze it, poke your fingers in it? What does it sound like as you walk or stamp in it? What does it sound like when you shake the snow off branches, and throw it at the wall or fence? Can you smell snow? As you sniff the air, what can you smell? Why? Is it a good idea to taste snow? Why not? What do you think it would taste like? (Make sure they do not try it!)

Follow-up activities

✧ Repeat the sensory snow exercise a few days later with 'old' snow.
✧ Look at snowflakes through a microscope and describe what can be seen. They could then make snowflakes by folding and cutting paper.
✧ Read the poem 'It's snowed' on page 71. Encourage the children to talk about their own experiences of stamping in the snow, building a snowman, sledging, rolling in the snow and snowballing.
✧ The children can make a collage of a snow scene, using cotton wool, glitter and so on.

SNOWMEN BISCUITS

Objective

Mathematics – to practise weighing and measuring cookery ingredients.

Group size

Up to four children.

What you need

Plastic tablecloth, aprons (one for each child), snowmen-shaped biscuit cutters, two baking trays, weighing scales, mixing bowl, wooden spoon, individual boards, rolling pins, tablespoon, knife, palette knife, measuring jug, wire rack, 50g caster sugar, 175g plain flour, 125g softened butter, a tablespoon of milk, icing sugar for 'dusting', red liquorice 'laces', chocolate drops, glacé cherries, large sheet of paper, felt-tipped pen.

Preparation

Make a simple pictorial recipe chart on the sheet of paper. Place the utensils on one side of the table and the ingredients on the other. Set the oven to 350°F/180°C/gas mark 4.

What to do

Ensure that the children wash their hands and each put on an apron. Introduce the utensils one at a time and see if the children can name them and work out their use. Read through the recipe chart aloud with the children and let them take turns to weigh all the ingredients into the mixing bowl. Weigh the softened butter before letting the children chop it up, and then weigh it again, to show that the weight has not changed. Let the children sieve the flour, and help rub the ingredients together with their fingertips, until the mixture resembles breadcrumbs. Add the milk, and bind everything together to make a ball of dough.

Divide the dough between the children, and let them roll it out and use their cutter to each make one or more 'snowmen', depending on the size of the cutter. Let the children help grease the baking trays, and bake the biscuits for about twenty minutes until cooked. When they are cooled the children can dust them with icing sugar and decorate them, using liquorice for lips, a glacé cherry for the nose, and chocolate drops for eyes and buttons.

Discussion

How is the flour different after it has been sieved? How many lumps of dough should we divide this ball into? How are we going to make the lumps flat? How many biscuits do you think you can each make with your dough?

Follow-up activities

✧ Make 'instant' snowmen using ice-cream and a scoop. Use two 'scoops' for each snowman and decorate in the same way as the biscuits.
✧ Make ice-lollies using fruit juice, and make a chart showing everyone's favourite flavour.

SNOWMEN PAIRS

Objective

Mathematics – to look carefully at detail and to match pairs.

Group size

Up to twenty children.

What you need

Card, felt-tipped pens/crayons, scissors, string, adhesive tape, cassette recorder and dancing music, space to dance in.

Preparation

Make ten different pairs of card snowmen, each about 40cm high, altering details such as colour of eyes, shape of noses, number of buttons, patterns on hats and scarves. Using adhesive tape, stick a length of string (70cm) in a loop, to the bottom of each snowman, so that the children can wear their 'upside down' snowman round their necks. When a child holds his/her snowman, it will appear upright to the child.

What to do

Hold up the ten different snowmen one at a time and ask the children to describe each one aloud. Then hold up a second snowman next to the first and ask whether they are the same or different.

Give each child a snowman 'necklace' to wear. Play the music and tell the children to dance around. When the music stops each child must find their matching partner who is wearing the corresponding picture, to make a pair of snowmen. They can then sit down together.

When all the children are sitting down in pairs, let the children exchange 'necklaces' with others, and the game can start again.

Discussion

Can you find a snowman with the same coloured eyes as yours? Is there another snowman wearing a scarf with the same pattern as yours? Can you see another snowman with the same number of buttons as yours?

Follow-up activities

✧ Give each child a copy of photocopiable page 92 and ask them to add details to the snowmen on the right hand side of the page to make the pairs of snowmen look the same.

✧ Give one card snowman each to ten children, and ask them to stand side-by-side in a line, while everyone recites the poem, 'Ten white snowmen' on page 72. Each 'snowman' should 'disappear' appropriately according to the rhyme.

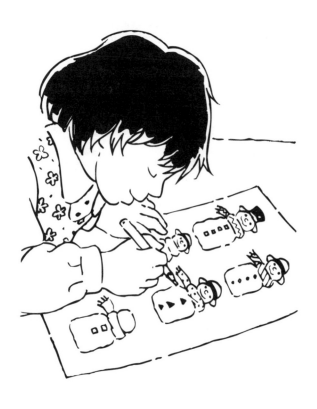

TRACKS IN THE SNOW

Objective

PE – to move like hibernating animals, searching for food in the snow.

Group size

Up to ten children.

What you need

A large white double bed sheet, white card and paper, black felt-tipped pen, scissors, clear plastic film, black sugar paper, small pictures or drawings of nuts, berries, insects and slugs, a shopping basket.

Preparation

Copy out the chart (below) on to a large piece of paper. Copy each set of animal tracks from the chart on to separate pieces of paper. For the snake 'track', cut a piece of paper 50cm x 10cm and draw the imprint of the underside of a snake in the 'snow'. Cut out each set of tracks and the 'snake' track, mount on card, and cover with clear plastic film. Cut out ten pairs of 'farmer's boot prints' from black sugar paper. Tell the children about animals which hibernate. Explain that no animals actually sleep continuously for the whole winter, but that they wake up every few weeks to go in search of food before going to sleep again. Tell the children that if this happens in snowy weather, the animals' tracks may be seen. Spread the bed sheet on the floor.

What to do

One child is chosen to be the 'kind farmer'. She or he is given the basket of 'food' pictures and should turn around, or leave the room, until it is time to be recalled to the game. Each child chooses to be an animal – a hedgehog, squirrel, dormouse, frog or snake. At each child's 'turn', s/he curls up under a corner of the sheet 'hibernating under the snow'. The child should be holding the 'track' cards.

After a few moments, the child 'wakes up', and moves appropriately across the sheet, in search of food, placing the 'track' cards on the sheet, as s/he moves. The 'animal' does not find any food, however. The kind farmer is now recalled. The animal, 'afraid of all people', hides under a corner of the sheet trying not to disturb the 'tracks'. The farmer must work out, from the 'tracks' and the chart, which animal is hiding. The farmer then brings out the appropriate 'food' picture from the basket, puts it on the 'snow' and leaves, making 'footprints' on the way. The animal emerges and eats the 'food'. The farmer now becomes an animal, and chooses another child to be the 'farmer.'

Discussion

How does each animal move? Which one dashes and darts, and which one slithers and slides? Who 'shuffles' slowly, and who 'scuttles' quickly? Which one springs and leaps in the air?

Follow-up activities

✧ Let the children make shoe and boot prints in damp soil or sand.
✧ Use potato prints to make 'animal track' pictures.
✧ Read the poem 'Hibernating hedgehog' on page 72, and sing the song 'Snowy footprints' on page 82. Encourage the children to make up further verses about various 'snowy footprints'.

EXPLORERS!

Objective

History – to learn about the bravery of polar explorers.

Group size

Five children at a time.

What you need

Three sledges, 'provisions' and 'fuel' (could be wooden bricks to weigh down the sledges), warm outdoor clothing, small tent, six skipping ropes, a compass, pictures of polar expeditions, a globe.

Preparation

Tell the whole group about the North Pole (Arctic) and the South Pole (Antarctic) and show them both locations on the globe. Briefly tell the children that Captain Robert Falcon Scott (or 'Scott of the Antarctic') wanted to be the first man to explore the South Pole, and how difficult this was then (1912), and still is now. Tell them that Scott started out on his expedition with eleven other men, motorised sledges and ponies and dogs to pull the other sledges. Explain that it was so cold that seven of the men went home, along with the ponies and dogs, the motorised sledges broke down and that the five men still left had to pull three sledges between them. Explain how disappointed they felt when they realised that another expedition, (led by Amundsen) had reached the South Pole just before they did. Say that they suffered in the terrible blizzards and that sadly all five men, including Scott, died because of the cold, on the way home. Explain how brave they were and that Scott's diary was very important to scientists who knew very little about the South Pole until he and his expedition went there.

What to do

Tell the children that in groups of five they may go out in the snow (with a helper) to try and do some of the things that a polar expedition must do. Make sure the children going out have warm coats and gloves and make sure that you limit the time any child is allowed to stay outside in the cold.

Let the children tie two ropes to each sledge, and fill each one with 'provisions' and 'fuel', including the tent. Two groups of children can work in pairs pulling a sledge between them, leaving one child on his/her own with the third sledge. Let them pull the sledges along and 'make camp', setting up the tent, making a 'fire' outside it, cooking 'food' on it and pretending to 'sleep' in the tent, just for a moment!

Discussion

Can you move quickly in the snow? How can you make it fair for the single third person pulling the sledge alone? How do you know that you are going in the right direction? Do you think you could keep moving in a blizzard?

Follow-up activities

✧ Discuss the dangers that other sorts of explorers face in certain weather conditions such as mountain climbers, who have to be very careful in a white-out (a blizzard) and who must take shelter until the blizzard dies down.
✧ Tell the children about present day explorers, such as Sir Ranulph Fiennes, who still travel to cold places and climb high mountains to find out more.

SNOWY NIGHT PICTURES

Objective

Art — to recreate a 'snowy night' scene using 'snowy paint'.

Group size

Up to ten.

What you need

Black and dark blue sugar paper, scissors, yellow sticky backed paper, flour, jug of water, white paint, mixing bowl, large spoon, saucers, felt-tipped pens, paintbrushes, toy cars.

Preparation

Let the children cut out simple building shapes from black sugar paper (houses, flats, shops, churches), helping them as necessary. Set out a table with the mixing bowl, flour, white paint, jug of water and spoon on.

What to do

Let the children help you mix together the flour, paint and water. Empty some flour into the bowl and ask the children to take turns to pour in a little water at a time, stirring all the time. Add white powder paint little by little until you have a thin mixture.

Help the children to stick their black buildings onto pieces of dark blue paper, adding yellow 'lit up' windows. Older children could use felt-tipped pens to draw tiny details inside the windows (Christmas trees, faces and so on). Ask the children to spoon some of the 'snowy paint' on to saucers, to dip their brushes in it, and use it to make snowflakes and 'fallen snow' at the bottom of their pictures. They could even use a toy car to push across the 'snowy paint' leaving 'tyre marks'.

Discussion

Ask the children if they have ever been on a night-time walk when it has been snowing, and have looked in at windows. Have they noticed how quiet everything becomes, because the snow muffles a lot of noise? Have they ever walked in slushy snow that has started to melt? What do we need to wear on our feet to avoid getting them wet?

Follow-up activities

✧ Let each child paint a large Christmas tree on dark blue paper, using fluorescent paint for the decorations. Cut out some people from magazines or catalogues and stick them around the tree.
✧ Cut doilies into small circles to use as stencils, for 'snowflakes'. Apply white paint with brushes, through the stencils on to dark paper. Add silver glitter to make night-time snowflake pictures.
✧ Read the poem 'Jack Frost' on page 73.

IT'S COLD HERE!

Objective

Geography — to find out about the dangers of icebergs.

Group size

Up to six children around the water tray.

What you need

Water tray, small polythene sandwich bags and tie tags, water, toy boats, play people, pictures of icebergs, access to a freezer, sticky labels, a pen.

Preparation

Make 'icebergs' by filling small sandwich bags with water, securing them with tie tags and placing them in a freezer. Fill the water tray.

What to do

Look at pictures and photographs of icebergs in the Arctic and Atlantic Oceans. Peel off the bags from the frozen 'icebergs' and put them in the water tray. Specify how many passengers should go in the 'ship', possibly with number labels.

Let the children guide the ships on a journey past the icebergs. Can they reach the other side of the water tray in safety? Warn the children not to put their fingers on the 'icebergs' for extended periods or they will 'burn' their skin.

Discussion

Discuss what would happen to the 'ships' if they hit an iceberg. Talk about the instrument panel and radar on the ship that warns the captain if there is an obstruction in the water. Discuss how only one third of the iceberg can be seen above the water with two thirds out of sight. How do the ships contact the outside world when an iceberg has been struck?

Follow-up activities

✧ Let them make little lifeboats for the big ships out of small polystyrene food trays. Help the play people to 'climb' over the sides of the ships down to the lifeboats when an iceberg has been struck.
✧ Explain the meaning of the terms 'ice-caps', and point out that the North Pole (Arctic) is covered by an ice-cap, as is the South Pole (Antarctic). Explain that the tops of mountains can also be covered in ice-caps.
✧ Look at pictures of real lifeboats. Discuss other ways of being rescued at sea (helicopter and so on).

SLIPPING AND SLIDING

Objective

Science – to find that some substances provide a surface grip and stop ice being slippery.

Group size

Up to five children.

What you need

Patch of ice on a cold winter's day (pour some cold water onto a controlled area), five foil pie plates, a tablespoon each of sand, salt, flour and sugar, tablespoon of milk in a dish, jug of water, tray.

Preparation

The night before you wish to do the activity, pour water into each pie plate and leave out overnight to freeze. Next day, put a tablespoon each of sand, salt, flour and sugar on a tray, together with a dish of milk. Dress the children in warm clothes, ready to go outside.

What to do

Let each child have a carefully supervised slide on a patch of ice, one at a time. Take extreme care that the children are well supervised to prevent falls or injury. Show the children the five frozen plates and ask each child to sprinkle a different substance on

each pie plate, leave them, and return later to see what has happened.

You should see that the plates with the flour and sugar have been unaffected, but that the ice on the plates with the sand and salt has started to melt and break up. The milk will have frozen on top of the existing ice on the plate.

Discussion

Talk about how, although it is fun to slide on ice patches, it can be dangerous, especially for old people who might fall and break their bones, and for vehicles, which may skid and crash. Tell the children that we sometimes cannot wait for the ice to melt and must put something on the ice to make it less slippery. When the children have returned to examine the plates, ask which ones are the least slippery – why? What has happened to the plate with milk in it? Have the children noticed salt containers at roadsides? Talk about 'gritter' lorries. Talk about the extreme dangers of walking on frozen ponds.

Follow-up activities

✧ Investigate which type of shoes or boots has the best grip on slippery ice.
✧ Leave a washing-up bowl filled with water outside overnight to freeze. The next day, add play people and a 'Danger! Thin Ice!' sign and let the children play out a 'rescue' scenario.

CHAPTER 6
THE EFFECTS OF THE WEATHER

This chapter takes the children 'around the world' to investigate the effects of the weather on birds and animals in other countries. They can find out how sports and living conditions vary according to extreme weather conditions.

THE TIME OF YEAR

Objective

Mathematics – to sort pictures into 'seasonal' sets.

Group size

Up to eight children.

What you need

A washing line, four pegs, four large sheets of paper, felt-tipped pen, cards showing seasonal occurrences, for example: spring (crocuses, birds building nests, lambs gambolling); summer (butterflies, fledglings hatching, tadpoles); autumn (hedgehogs looking for food in preparation for hibernating, sycamore 'keys', farmers harvesting crops); winter (a bird table, animals hibernating). A tray, a cassette recorder and tape, eight chairs.

Preparation

Write 'Spring', 'Summer', 'Autumn' and ' Winter' at the top of the sheets of paper and below each title draw a large tree appropriate to the season for example, a spring tree in bud, a summer tree with green leaves, an autumn tree with brown leaves

falling down and a winter tree with no leaves. Hang up the tree pictures on the line with pegs. Arrange the chairs in a circle, facing outwards. Spread some of the picture cards face downwards on a tray.

What to do

Play the music tape and ask the children to dance around the chairs to the music. When the music stops the children must sit on the chairs.

You can then choose one child, who stands up and selects a card from the tray. The child must describe what is happening in the chosen picture, what the weather is like, and the time of year it is taking place. The child then places the card underneath the appropriate 'tree' picture hanging on the line to sort it into the correct season.

Discussion

Talk about the seasons of the year, and the different kinds of weather associated with each season. Why don't we see many flowers in the winter? Why is it a good idea to feed the birds in winter, but not in summer?

Follow-up activities

✧ Let the children colour and cut out the four 'seasonal' trees on the photocopiable page 93, and stick them on card. Put the trees together and create 'seasonal' scenarios using play figures, cotton wool 'snow' and so on.

✧ Substitute seasonal objects for the cards on the tray — a kite for a windy spring day, a pair of sunglasses for the summer, a small rake for raking up autumn leaves, and a bird feeder for feeding birds in winter-time.

✧ See if the children can suggest a season for each verse of 'Going, going, gone!' by Judith Nicholls, on page 71.

TODAY'S WEATHER IS ...

Objective

English — to encourage the children to speak in front of an audience.

Group size

One at a time, in front of an audience.

What you need

Large sheet of paper, felt-tipped pens, easel (or wall space), Blu-Tack, white card, scissors, newspaper weather reports, video excerpts of TV weather reports, girls' and boys' 'smart' clothes (jacket, bow-tie).

Preparation

Draw a simple outline of the British Isles (see below) on the paper. Cut out six cards (10cm square) and draw the weather symbols on them (see below). Attach a piece of Blu-Tack to the back of each card. Fix the map to the easel or wall space.

What to do

If possible, show the children the video clip of the weather report. Look at the newspaper weather reports together and show the map to the children pointing out your home town/city, as well as England, Scotland, Wales and Ireland and perhaps, London. Hold up and explain the weather symbols.

Now ask for a volunteer to give the weather report for today. Let your volunteer put on a smart jacket and stand at the easel to demonstrate the weather! Encourage any children willing to have a go by prompting them where necessary. If any children are reluctant to be in the spotlight don't make them perform, instead ask them some simple questions to encourage a contribution.

Discussion

Explain that the weather isn't the same in all parts of the same country. Talk about visiting family and friends in other parts of the country and experiencing different weather. Talk about why we need to know about the weather before going on a long car journey to estimate how long the journey will take, or if there will be traffic jams and so on.

Follow-up activities

✧ Use the photocopiable sheet on page 94 to give the children practice in recognising weather symbols.
✧ Arrange motorway traffic jams on the floor road mat and have a traffic police helicopter pilot surveying the scene from above (sitting in a 'helicopter' — an old highchair, minus front tray). The pilot, using a 'radio phone' communicates with police-officers on the ground who put up new signs, redirect traffic down other roads, attend to crashes and chase criminals!
✧ Read the poem 'The shirts on the line' by John Foster on page 68.

TOO COLD!

Objective

PE – to recreate the stop-go journey of the swallow as it migrates.

Group size

Up to six children.

What you need

Masking tape, card, felt-tipped pens, a tambour, wood blocks, a tambourine, maracas, pictures of swallows, a world map.

Preparation

Stick a long line of masking tape across as large an expanse of floor as possible. Make two arrow shapes with the tape at both ends of the line. Write 'north' and 'south' on two cards, and stick them at either end of the masking tape next to the arrow points. Tell the children how in autumn some birds, such as swallows fly away from Great Britain because it will be too cold for them to stay for the winter in this country. The insects that swallows eat all die in the winter, and so the swallows would have no food. Tell the children that Great Britain is in the 'north of the world', but that Africa is 'towards the south'. When the swallows all fly away from Great Britain they migrate to the south, to Africa. Tell the children that they all try to fly back again to Great Britain in the spring-time.

What to do

Tell the children that they are the 'swallows' and to line up in 'Great Britain' at the 'north' end of the tape. Tell them to listen carefully while you play some percussion instruments which will tell them what the weather is like. To denote a 'following wind', during which the 'swallows' can make good progress you will play the tambour, by rotating your palm around it. Sudden bursts on the wood blocks represent being 'blown off course', and the 'swallows' must move accordingly. A tambourine could represent a 'storm at sea', while the maracas could be a sandstorm in the desert. The 'swallows' must fly towards the 'south' or stand still, according to the 'weather sounds' they hear. Finally they can fly back home in the spring.

Discussion

If the swallows meet a 'following wind' is that good or bad for them? Why? What does it mean if they are 'blown off course'? Have you ever seen birds lining up ready to fly south? How do animals know where to go? (Parents, instinct, the sun and so on.)

Follow-up activities

✧ Tell the children about other birds and animals which migrate, for example: the Arctic tern which travels 11,000 miles from its summer home in North America to Antarctica where it stays all winter; and wildebeest who move in their thousands in the African dry season, to find fresh grass.

✧ Sing the song 'Just like the birds do' by Clive Barnwell on page 83.

A WORLD CRUISE

Objective

Geography — to find out about climates in different countries.

Group size

Up to five children.

What you need

A large world map, a wheeled vehicle to serve as a 'cruise ship' (a sit-and-ride truck / tricycle), travel agents' cruise brochures, two small shoulder bags, card, felt-tipped pens, scissors, adhesive tape, Blu-Tack, colour postcards (or hand-drawn pictures of climates in different countries, such as snow in Switzerland, sun in the Caribbean), pair of sunglasses, a child's 'parasol', ski gloves, mask, tray, sea music, an area of floor space, four chairs, cassette player.

Preparation

Fix the map to a wall at the side of the floor space. Arrange the chairs side-by-side at right-angles to the map. Draw and cut out a 'cruise ship' making the top approximately 40cm long, and the bottom 30cm long (see diagram), from card. Attach this to one of the shoulder bags with adhesive tape so that if a child puts the bag over his / her shoulder and sits on the wheeled vehicle, she / he will appear to be a 'passenger' on a 'cruise ship'. Put the sunglasses, gloves, parasol and mask in the other shoulder bag.

What to do

Ask for a volunteer 'passenger', who puts the 'ship-bag' over one shoulder, with the other bag across the other shoulder, and sits on the tricycle ready to 'sail' around the world. You can then hold up the postcards / hand-drawn cards and talk about the countries they represent, and the country's weather. Point to the countries on the map and hold up the relevant items from the second shoulder bag, such as a pair of sunglasses for Spain, the ski-gloves for Switzerland, the parasol for India and so on.

The 'voyage' may now begin, with the children sitting on chairs at the 'quay side' waving off the 'passenger' who can wave and make two hooting sounds. The 'cruise ship' then sails around the world while you play the 'sea music', and stops when the music stops. You can now offer the 'passenger' a tray with the postcards / hand-drawn cards on, face down. The child picks a card, tries to name the country and the weather, and, if possible, to point to the country on the map. The child can then select the relevant item from the second 'travel bag' before 'disembarking' so another child may have a turn.

Discussion

Talk about how different countries have different kinds of weather. Perhaps some of the children have spoken on the telephone to relatives abroad who are experiencing different weather from our own? Have any children been on holiday somewhere where the weather is very different to Great Britain or different at other times of year (such as Australia during our winter)? Does the weather vary between different parts of Great Britain?

Follow-up activities

✧ Play 'Travel agents' — encouraging the children to talk about the relevant climates of each country they wish to visit, and to think about the appropriate clothing, pointing to their destination on the map.
✧ Using the tray of postcards / hand-drawn cards, play at shopping for clothes for different countries. A child selects a card and has to choose appropriate clothes from the following 'shops' — shoe shop (ski boots, beach sandals, Wellingtons, mountain boots); hat shop (sun hat, rain hat, ski / mountaineering bobble hat); clothes shop (anorak with furry hood for Arctic expeditions, swimming trunks / costume, rain coat, ski suit).

A STRONG HOUSE

Objective

Design and technology – to design a weatherproof house for a cold, damp country.

Group size

Up to four children.

What you need

Large cardboard cartons, parcel tape, scissors, large drinking straws, Blu-Tack, white corrugated paper from food packaging, cotton wool, scraps of carpet, card. Double-glazing, cavity wall insulation and solar heating brochures, polythene wallets for storing paper, camera and film.

Preparation

Take photographs of your own house to show features designed to keep cold and dampness out such as guttering and drain pipes, lagged pipes in a garage, lagging in the loft and around the hot water cistern, radiators, carpets, draught excluders, a porch and so on.

What to do

Tell the children that in Great Britain homes are built to keep coldness and dampness out. Show the children the photographs and brochures and

discuss them, asking the children whether they have similar features in their homes.

Let the children use the cartons to build a house, incorporating the features you have discussed. Use straws attached with Blu-Tack for 'drain-pipes', cotton wool 'lagging', corrugated paper for radiators, double-thickness polythene wallets for 'double glazing' and cardboard strips for the 'draught excluders'.

Discussion

When the rain falls on your roof, where does it go? Why do we 'lag' pipes? What is inside radiators? How can we stop rain and cold winds rushing inside our house when we open the door?

Follow-up activities

✧ Talk to the children about houses in hot countries which try to keep the heat out. Do they know how this is done? (By painting walls white to reflect the heat of the sun, putting up shutters, fly-screens, cool tiled floors).
✧ Talk about how birds try to make their nests as strong and as weatherproof as possible. If possible bring an abandoned nest in for the children to see (wear gloves when you handle it and do not allow the children to touch it).
✧ Add 'weatherproofing' features to dolls' houses.

SPORTY WEATHER

Objective

PE — to practise sporting body movements for different kinds of weather.

What you need

Poster depicting a wide variety of sports, sports equipment (tennis racket, golf club, football, cricket bat), hamper.

Preparation

Place all the sports equipment in a large hamper. Display the sports poster at child height. Clear a large space for the children and ask them to take off shoes and socks. (Older children could change to PE clothes.)

What to do

Ask an individual child to pick an item of equipment from the hamper and see if he/she can name the sport it is used in and name the equipment. Can the child match the equipment with a picture on the sports poster?

Ask all the children to mime the action of the sport copying a child at the front (or an adult for difficult sports such as golf). Name the action as it is performed, for example forehand, backhand and serve in tennis.

Discussion

Can the children name the appropriate weather for each sport? Are there certain sports that can be played in any weather because they are played indoors? (Basketball and ice hockey.) Can the children think of sports that can be played indoors or outdoors, for example tennis, football, swimming? Which sports suit cold snowy weather? (Skiing, snow boarding.) Which sports suit windy weather? (Sailing and windsurfing.) Which sports are best enjoyed in sunny weather? (Swimming in the sea.)

Follow-up activities

✧ Invite visitors in to demonstrate more unusual sports and related equipment such as fencing.
✧ How many different ball games can the children think of? Make a display linking balls to their related sports — include football, cricket, table tennis, rugby, basketball and tennis.
✧ Complete the photocopiable sheet on page 95 to reinforce the activity.

A SUNNY SMILE

Objective

English – to find out how people's moods can be affected by the weather.

Group size

Whole group.

What you need

Pictures of children showing different facial expressions (angry, crying, smiling, puzzled), pictures of the environment under various weather conditions (sunny day, stormy day, foggy day and rainy day), two small easels, Blu-Tack.

Preparation

Attach the pictures of facial expressions on to a small easel to one side of your chair. Attach the pictures of different kinds of weather to the other easel and place this on the other side of your chair. Sit in your chair and gather the children together in front of the easels.

What to do

Ask individual children to try and match a picture of a facial expression with a type of weather. Bear in mind that no answer will be completely right or wrong. Some children might feel very happy in rainy weather because they like splashing in puddles while others are bored because they have to stay in, some might enjoy the excitement of thunder and lightning while others are frightened by it.

Encourage the other children to describe the faces which the child is assuming and to use descriptive language.

Discussion

When do you have a sunny smile? What things do you do on a sunny day which make you happy? Have you ever cried tears as big as rain drops? Why? Have you ever 'burst into tears', like a rain cloud? Have you seen anyone 'look like thunder'? Why were they so angry? Have you ever been 'in a fog'? Why was that? Have you ever felt 'all at sea'? What made you feel like that?

Follow-up activities

✧ Make drawings showing certain expressions related to different types of weather such as crying teardrops on a rainy day.
✧ Read the story *Angry Arthur* by Hiawyn Oram (Red Fox) in which Arthur's anger is like the escalation of a storm from thunder and lightning to a 'universe quake'. Ask the children if they have ever had tantrums about something small, after having been in a bad mood – just like thunder 'brewing'?

WHEN THE WEATHER GOES WRONG

Objective

RE — to be aware of people whose lives are adversely affected by severe weather conditions.

Preparation

Tell the children that sometimes very extreme weather can make people's lives very difficult in some countries. Explain that when this happens these people need the help of people from around the world. Talk about the effects of drought, famine, floods and hurricanes.

What to do

Choose different children to act out the roles of people experiencing problems because of adverse weather conditions.

You should introduce each 'scenario' and ask the audience to describe what might happen with the severe weather and to suggest ways of helping. For example, you could show a person walking a very long distance with a bucket to get some dirty water for his/her family; a mother and father and baby (doll) completely running out of water; a family whose house has been flooded and a family whose house has been damaged by a hurricane.

Discussion

Is it right for a person to have to walk a long way for water? If the water is dirty, what might happen? What can we do to help? Is it a good idea to send money? What should we send instead? Who will send it? Can a family cook food without water? Can they wash themselves? What could happen if they don't? Can they grow food of their own without water? What should we send to families who lose their homes in floods or hurricanes?

Follow-up activities

✧ Invite a representative from an international charity to talk to the children about self-help projects in developing countries.
✧ Talk to the children about how they could raise money for international causes: organise a sale of toys or clothes or collect them and take them to a charity shop.
✧ Emphasise the lives of children in developing countries and, as a group, sponsor a child.

CHAPTER 7
DISPLAYS

Displays can extend children's learning, reinforce their feelings of 'ownership' and self-esteem, and are informative for parents and visitors. This chapter gives general ideas on presentation, as well as ideas for four specific displays.

MAKING DISPLAYS

Displaying the children's work demonstrates that it has a value and that it is appreciated. It gives parents and visitors a chance to learn more about what is happening in your group on a day-to-day basis and offers the children an opportunity to explain their work to friends and family. Displays act as a focal point, encouraging conversations among groups of children as they proudly point out their individual contributions, furthering enthusiasm for the current topic.

Displays will also brighten up your room. However, it is important that they should be easy to assemble, not take too long and should involve the children themselves. There is no educational value in asking children to simply draw round stencils or colour in cut-out pictures when they could be using their extensive imaginations and talents to create their own unique work. Enhance this work on occasions by double-mounting and cutting round the edges of the pictures leaving a thin edge. The children can also help to create unusual display backing and borders by using techniques such as potato printing, rubbings and finger painting.

Add interest using textured paper, draped materials, abstract wrapping paper, shiny foil and crêpe paper. Display work at different levels to allow the children to handle objects and take part in interactive activities – they will enjoy having flaps to open, different textures to touch and simple instructions to follow. Use thick felt-tipped pens to label displays in large letters which can be seen from across the room. Either make a felt-tipped pen margin half a centimetre in from the edge of the label or mount it on a contrasting colour before attaching it to the display. Try and make the shape and colour of your lettering, and even the shape of the whole display, link in with the theme that is being used.

SUN SAFETY

What you need

Children's sun-glasses, T-shirt, sun lotion, lip sun block, sun-hat, bright yellow and orange sugar paper, potatoes, gold foil/pen, two large shallow trays, sand, water, small brightly coloured or stripy flannels (towels for the play people), dolls/play people, children's home-made boats, cocktail parasols, stapler, adhesive, yellow and blue cloths, table in front of the display board.

Preparation

Fill one tray with sand and the other with water and place them on the table — the sand tray on top of a yellow cloth and the water tray on top of a blue cloth. Trickle sand over the edge of the sand tray to make it look like a sand dune.

What to do

Staple bright yellow backing paper onto the display board, cut out strips of a contrasting colour such as orange and ask the children to print a sun border on the orange paper using cut potatoes. Attach a bright sun with the words 'Sun safety' in gold coloured writing.

Remind the children about the items needed to keep safe in the sunshine. Pick up the sun-glasses, sun-hat, sun lotion, T-shirt and lip sun block one at a time asking the children why they are necessary and which part of the body they protect. Attach the items to the display board with the children watching. You may need to staple cardboard shelves to the board for the empty sun lotion bottle and the sun-glasses. Ask the children for suggestions for captions for the display.

Give the children the flannels, parasols and play people and ask them to arrange them in the sand tray 'beach'. Ask them to float their boats on the 'sea'. Complete the scene by making little paper sun hats for the play people on the beach.

Discussion

Why do we need to protect ourselves against the sun? How can we do this? How can we keep cool when it's very sunny? If we are nice and cool when we're in the sea, do we still need to protect ourselves against the sun?

RAINY DAY WELLIES

What you need

Coloured sugar paper, paints, paintbrushes, pencil, coloured Cellophane, coloured sticky paper, four pairs of wellington boots in different sizes, foil, paper, adhesive, stapler, material cut into small pieces, buttons, wool, icing sugar, large box, large pieces of grey or green material.

Preparation

Prepare a collage table with materials, buttons and adhesive. Cut out silver foil puddles and cover the large box with 'raindrop' paper. Place one of each pair of boots in the box.

What to do

Draw around four children lying down on sugar paper. Cut out the outlines and let the children use the collage materials to make clothes, the wool to make hair and to paint faces on the life-size models.

When these are dry, add Cellophane raincoats and sticky paper wellington boots, matching the colour and design to those on the real wellington boots.

Ask the children to paint the backing paper with a thin icing sugar solution using large brushes. Immediately drip watery paint onto the paper to give the impression of soft focus rain drops. Staple the backing paper and collage figures to the display board when dry. Ask the children to paint large umbrellas, one for each collage figure, and cut them out leaving a small border — add to the display. Cover the table in grey or green material, and staple down the silver foil puddles. Put one boot on each puddle. Write labels inviting the children to take a boot from the box and match it to its pair.

Discussion

Can the children put the boots in order of size? Have they got their own umbrellas? Can they describe the pictures or patterns on their own umbrellas? What are their raincoats like — are they see-through like the Cellophane ones?

Icing sugar solution with paint dripped on

painted umbrellas

collage clothes

Cellophane rain coats

sticky paper boots

silver foil puddle

box of wellingtons

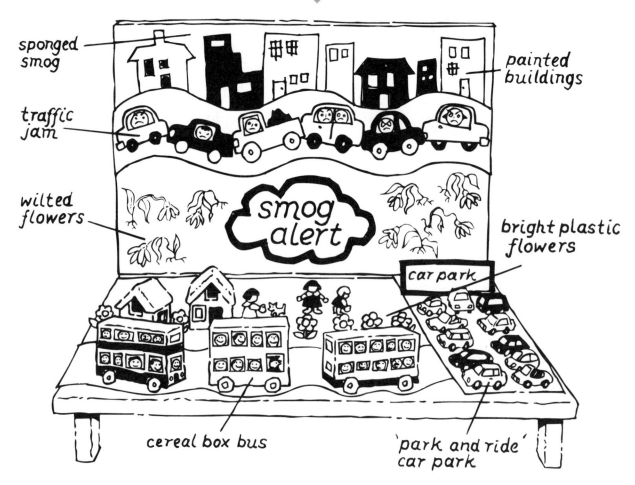

sponged smog

painted buildings

traffic jam

wilted flowers

smog alert

bright plastic flowers

car park

cereal box bus

'park and ride' car park

SMOG ALERT

What you need

Grey and green sugar paper, paints, grey wool, white sugar paper, crayons, three cereal packets, circles of card, toy cars, small sponges, bunch of wilted flowers, garage, brightly coloured plastic flowers, play houses, stapler, card, play people.

Preparation

Prepare small sponges and grey/white paint. Cut out two long grey roads from the sugar paper. Cover the table with green sugar paper. Write and mount the sign 'Smog alert'.

What to do

Ask the children to sponge the grey paint on to the backing paper explaining that the colour represents all the smoke and exhaust fumes in the atmosphere. Let the children paint buildings and vehicles, adding crayoned sad faces on squares of white paper in each car once the paint is dry. Pin

or staple the sponged backing paper on to the display board, and add the cut-out buildings, one of the grey road strips, the nose-to-tail traffic jam and the wilted flowers at the road side. Sponge some of the grey/white smog on the houses.

Make three buses out of cereal packets using circles of card for the wheels and crayoned happy faces on squares of white paper for the windows. Stick down the other grey road, position small play houses along the side of it. When the buses are dry, position them along the road with a large car park at the right hand side of the table full of toy cars. Attach a large sign to the car park 'Park and ride'. Position the brightly coloured plastic flowers along the roadway. Add a few painted cyclists and play people pedestrians.

Discussion

Why do the children think everyone in the traffic jam looks so miserable and the people on the buses look much happier? Why are the flowers wilting near the busy road? Remind the children about the discussion they had during the 'Smog' activity on page 42.

MY FAVOURITE WEATHER

What you need

Coloured backing paper, thick felt-tipped pen, coloured felt-tipped pens, white circles of paper about 5cm diameter, paints, painting paper, aprons, white paper, collage materials (wool, ribbons and shiny coloured paper).

Preparation

Make a pictogram chart divided into columns headed: 'Sunny, Foggy, Rainy, Snowy, and Stormy' with relevant illustrations, under the headings. Leave space for children's paintings down the sides of the pictogram. Use a thick felt-tipped pen to write, 'My favourite weather' on a cloud shaped piece of white paper.

What to do

Show the children the pictogram headings and discuss which type of weather they like the best. Ask them to each paint a picture of what they like to do in their favourite weather. For example, they may choose snowy weather and paint a picture of building a snowman, or a storm and paint a picture of watching a storm through their windows. Double-mount the paintings and leave them to dry.

Give each child a circle and ask them to draw their own happy face using felt-tipped pens. Use collage materials for hair, ribbons and details such as hair slides. Ask the children to each place their individual faces in the column of their choice on the pictogram. Remind them that putting their smiley face in the sunny column means that they like sunny weather best and so on.

Position the pictogram in the middle of your display and arrange the paintings around the sides. Record how many like each kind of weather.

Discussion

Ask the children why they like or dislike each kind of weather. What do they most enjoy doing in any particular kind of weather? Is there anything the weather stops them from doing? Ask the children what it is like being outdoors in different kinds of weather; or indoors, watching it through a window; or thinking about it, snuggled up in bed.

Follow-up activities

✧ Cut out seasonal weather pictures from calendars. Discuss these with the children, jotting down what they say about them. Assemble the pictures and the children's words into booklets to hang on the 'Favourite weather' display.

✧ Stick pictures of people dressed for different weather onto paper and draw a weather background.

CHAPTER 8
ASSEMBLIES

This chapter suggests ideas for assemblies or group sharing times on the theme of 'Weather' and includes activities, prayers and songs.

ALL KINDS OF WEATHER

Giving thanks for all different kinds of weather is the theme of this assembly. It draws on previous experiences which children may have had during other activities particularly in science, language work and mathematics.

The children should have been encouraged to understand how fortunate they are to have such a generally balanced climate. They should be aware that people in some countries suffer from extremes of heat and cold and may also face floods or famine. This approach can lay the foundation for a future understanding of how different kinds of weather are necessary to sustain different forms of life.

Introduction

Let the children enter for the assembly while music such as 'Weather with you' by Crowded House or 'The rainy season' by Howard Devoto is played. Begin by encouraging them to recall different types of weather; record the suggestions on a flip chart, or use their own symbols on a weather chart. Other work could be presented by groups such as poems, songs and rhymes about the weather, and they could dress for different weather conditions.

Summarise by ensuring that the children have understood that different weather occurs around the world, which has different effects on people.

What to do

Invite a representative of each group of children to come into the centre and describe a different kind of weather – rainy, sunny, frosty. Encourage them to wear relevant clothing and to use any appropriate props such as umbrellas, sun creams and scarves.

Ask the children to highlight the advantages or disadvantages of their type of weather.

Reflection

Collect together some pictures of different weather scenes and hand these to the children. In a small gathering hand one out to each child present, or in a larger group divide the children into small groups. Ask the children to look at the pictures they have been given and to notice everything they can about them. Encourage them to reflect on the advantages and or disadvantages of the weather shown in their pictures. At this point, some children may be willing to share their reflections with the rest of the group.

Prayer

Some children may wish to thank God for the different types of weather – the rain and sunshine that help the plants to grow, the warmth that enables them to play outside, the beauty of the snow and ice and the refreshing coolness of the gentle breeze.

Song

As the children leave the gathering, play a recording of a popular song such as 'Walking on Sunshine' by Katrina and the Waves. Otherwise, choose a song from the selection in this book.

A WEATHER FABLE

The traditional fable *The North Wind and the Sun* (many versions available) is the theme of this assembly. It provides the opportunity for the children to explore the meaning of the story and the way in which different kinds of weather are used to represent human characteristics. The fierce wind symbolises bullying and roughness, while the sun symbolises the gentle art of persuasion.

Before the assembly begins make sure the children understand the different characteristics of the wind and sun. They should have heard stories, read poems and sung songs about the weather as well as looked at relevant pictures and photographs, and made lists of descriptive words about weather.

Introduction

Arrange two large spaces in the centre of the gathering — one to represent windy weather and one to represent sunny. Invite some children to stand in each space and to depict the main characteristics of the relevant type of weather. They can do this by singing or reciting rhymes or songs, showing artefacts and pictures, or by role-play or dancing (these will have to be prepared in advance).

Invite the children in the audience to think of some words to describe the two different kinds of weather. Write the children's responses on appropriately shaped pieces of card and place them in the two central areas.

What to do

Clear away the central area and introduce the story *The North Wind and the Sun*. You could either read it or tell it to the children, especially in a small group, but in a large gathering it may be better to have prepared some children to act it out using appropriate props and sound effects.

When you are telling the story, try to include the descriptive words which the children suggested to you earlier on.

Reflection

In silence, ask the children to think about the different ways in which the North Wind and the Sun both tried to make the man in the story remove his cloak. Remind the children that while the North Wind was strong it was also bossy and bold and the man became more determined to keep his cloak on. However the gentle and calming approach of the Sun was more successful, and in the end, the Sun achieved the desired goal.

Prayer

Create your own prayer about the ways in which people should treat those around them. Emphasise that bullying and brash boasting only creates ill-feeling, while gentle persuasion and kindness can lead to closer co-operation.

Some children may wish to ask God to help them and others to be kind, warm and gentle like the sun, rather than harsh and cruel like the wind.

Song

Play a recording of some soft and relaxing music or a song with a sunshine theme such as 'Here Comes the Sun' by The Beatles, as the children leave the gathering. Other 'sunshine' songs can also be found in this book.

SNOWFLAKES

The uniqueness of every snowflake is the focus for this assembly. It provides an opportunity to discuss how – like snowflakes – each person is individual and special, that no two people are exactly alike, but that everyone has qualities and skills of their own

Before the assembly takes place, the children should have been given the opportunity to learn as much as possible about snow. Dress some children as 'snowflakes'; each one should have a different and individual costume, perhaps of their own design.

Introduction

Invite the children to share their work on snow with each other. They could sing songs, recite poems and rhymes and look at pictures, posters, models and weather charts.

Some children may like to talk about playing in snowy weather and could role-play sledging, skiing and playing in the snow. Others may like to talk about disadvantages of snowy weather such as dangers to old people, or people on journeys and also the plight of birds or animals in search of food.

What to do

Arrange the children with a large space in the centre. Play a suitable piece of recorded music such as the soundtrack to 'The Snowman' (based on the book by Raymond Briggs) or Tchaikovsky's 'Dance of the Sugar Plum Fairy' from *The Nutcracker Suite*. Invite the 'snowflake' children to dance around, floating, rising, moving and swirling in all directions (you will need to prepare this and rehearse it in advance).

Encourage the children to notice the ways in which each snowflake looks and moves differently to the others; emphasise that although they are all different they are all beautiful.

Reflection

Ask the children to think for a few moments about the uniqueness of the 'snowflakes' they have seen. If it is possible look at some colour slides of real snowflakes under microscopes and encourage the children to notice their intricate patterns and designs. Play some background music while the children are thinking.

Prayer

End the gathering by encouraging the children to think of ways in which they too are all different and say a prayer thanking God for the diversity and beauty of creation. Compose this with the children, making reference to the particular skills and abilities of some of the children in your group.

Song

Play a recording of a popular song such as 'Winter Wonderland' (recorded by various artists) as the children leave the gathering. Alternatively, select a song from the 'Resources' section of this book.

Collective worship in schools

The assemblies outlined here are suitable for use with children in nurseries and playgroups, but would need to be adapted for use with pupils at registered schools. As a result of legislation enacted in 1944, 1988 and 1993, there are now specific points to be observed when developing a programme of Collective Acts of Worship in a school.

Further guidance will be available from your local SACRE – Standing Advisory Council for RE.

POEMS AND RHYMES

CAN YOU FEEL THE BEAT?
(A SUN CHANT)

Chorus
Can you feel the beat?
Can you feel the beat?
Can you feel the beat?
of the sun's hot heat?

All through the day the sun beats down
on field and forest and dusty town.

Chorus
Can you feel the beat? etc.

Yes, everything's dusty, hot and dry,
for the sun's rays sizzle from the bright blue sky.

Chorus
Can you feel the beat? etc.

Everything living, each leaf, each blade
is longing for water and looking for shade.

Chorus
Can you feel the beat? etc.

In the cool of the evening when the sun leaves the sky
everything living gives a long, deep sigh.

Chorus (NB altered)
Did you hear the beat? etc.

End: *Oh, yeah...!* (optional rallentando)

Tony Mitton

INCY WINCY

Incy Wincy spider
Climbed up the water spout.
Down came the rain
And washed the spider out.
Out came the sun
And dried up all the rain.
So Incy Wincy spider
Climbed up the spout again.

Traditional

PHOTOCOPIABLE RESOURCES

KEEPING COOL

In summer we wear
Cotton socks,
Cotton shorts
And cotton frocks.

That's because
Cotton's cool and thin.
It helps the air
Flow round our skin.

Cotton T-shirts
Keep us cool
and so does the water
In the padding pool!

John Foster

IF I WAS A RAINDROP

If I was a raindrop, where would I go?
Splat in the garden *(slap right leg)*
Splat on the path *(slap left leg)*
If I was a raindrop, where would I go?
Splat on the roof of your house!
(slap top of head with both hands)

If I was a hailstone, where would I go?
Rattle in the garden *(rat-tat-tat on right leg)*
Rattle on the path *(rat-tat-tat on left leg)*
If I was a hailstone, where would I go?
Rattle on the roof of your house!
(rat-tat-tat on head with both hands)

If I was snowflake, where would I go?
Soft in the garden *(rest hand softly on right leg)*
Soft on the path *(rest hand softly on left leg)*
If I was a snowflake, where would I go?
Soft on the roof of your house
(rest both hands on head)

If I was a sunbeam, where would I go?
Shine in the garden *(stroke right leg)*
Shine on the path *(stroke left leg)*
If I was a sunbeam, where would I go?
Shine on the roof of your house
(stroke head with both hands from top to smile)

Jan Jones

THE SHIRTS ON THE LINE

On a windy day
The shirts on the line
Wave their arms about
Dancing up and down.

On a sunny day
The shirts on the line
Stretch out
And sunbathe.

On a frosty day
The shirts on the line
Shiver and freeze
As stiff as statues.

On breezy days
The shirts on the line
Flap their arms
And whisper in the wind.

John Foster

THE COLOURS OF THE RAINBOW

RED — that's for danger — so don't cross the street;
ORANGE — like oranges, juicy and sweet;
YELLOW — the daffodils, bright as we pass;
GREEN is the colour of trees, leaves and grass;
BLUE makes me think of a clear, cloudless sky;
INDIGO's rich, like a deep purple dye;
VIOLET's a flower, a soft pinky-blue;
I love all the bright rainbow colours — don't you?

Sue Palmer

STORM SONG

(sung as a round to the tune of Frère Jacques)

I hear thunder
I hear thunder
Hark don't you?
Hark don't you?
Pitter, patter raindrops
Pitter, patter raindrops
I'm wet through
I'm wet through

Traditional

Second version:

I see lightning
I hear thunder
Rain on mud
Rain on mud
Oh, what a deluge!
Oh, what a deluge!
Now there's a flood
Now there's a flood

Susheila Stone

FOG

When I woke up
one winter day
the world had vanished
clean away.

I blinked, and wiped
the window pane.
I shook my head
and looked again.

I heard my little
brother shout,
'Hey! Someone's been
and rubbed it out!'

For all the world
was wrapped up tight
and muffled in
a mass of white.

'It's fog,' I heard
my mother say.
'The sun will clear it
all away.'

But I just stood
and stared in thrill
to see the world
so strange and still.

Tony Mitton

THE SAIL SONG

Blow, wind, blow.
Blow, wind, blow.
Come and sing your breezy song.
Come and blow my boat along.
Bring a gust (but not a gale!).
Come and fill my empty sail.
Blow, wind, blow.
Blow, wind, blow.

Puff, wind, puff.
Puff, wind, puff.
Puff me to a far off land
with coconuts and golden sand,
with skies of blue and shining sun
where days are long and full of fun,
where I can laze about and float
drifting in my little boat...
Puff, wind, puff.
Not *too* rough.
Yes, that's enough.
Puff, wind, puff.

Tony Mitton

WHAT IS FOG?

Puffs of dragon smoke
Curling round hedges and trees.

Clouds of steam from a giant's kettle
Pouring out over the city.

The breath from a dinosaur's nostrils
Blurring the world into a grey shadow.

John Foster

WEATHER HOUSE

Mr Weather: Our name is Mr and Mrs Weather
              But we never go out together.

Mrs Weather: I come out in the bright sunshine
              When the air is dry and the outlook is fine.

Mr Weather: When you see me, don't venture out yet.
              There's rain in the air and the forecast is wet.

Mrs Weather: Come in, Mr Weather, you don't like the sun —
              Go back out, Mr Weather, the rain has begun!

Sue Cowling

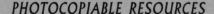

WIND FARM

There's a forest on the hillside
That isn't made of trees.
Dozens of windmills turn
Their faces to the breeze!

They have blades instead of branches
And they aren't even green
But they make light for the town
And our air stays clean!

Sue Cowling

GOING, GOING, GONE!

Holidays, camping out,
caravans, barbecues,
sandcastles, bicycling,
picnics and fun;
strawberries and icecream with
swimsuits and surfboards,
circuses, funfairs,
beaches and sun.

Cooler now,
back to school.
Autumn leaves
fall from trees,
sweaters out,
mittens on;
shadows grow,
Summer's gone.

Swallows go,
robins come;
frozen toes,
feet numb.
Ears sting,
eyes run,
red nose;
feel low.

Frost,
hail,
ice,

snow!

Judith Nicholls

IT'S SNOWED

It's snowed! It's snowed!
It's blocked the road.
The school is closed today!
Come on! Come on!
Get your wellies on!
We're going out to play.

We'll stamp footprints
In the snow
To show where we have been.
We'll build a snowman
In the park
Down beside the stream.

We'll get the sledge
Out of the shed
And go up by the mill.
We'll sit upright
And cling on tight
As we hurtle down the hill.

We'll roll about.
We'll laugh and shout,
And make snowballs to throw.
Come on! Come on!
Get your anorak on!
Come and play in the snow.

John Foster

TEN WHITE SNOWMEN

Ten white snowmen standing in a line,
One toppled over, then there were nine.

Nine white snowmen standing up straight,
One lost its balance, then there were eight.

Eight white snowmen in a snowy heaven,
The wind blew one over, then there were seven.

Seven white snowmen with pipes made of sticks,
One slumped to the ground, then there were six.

Six white snowmen standing by the drive,
One got knocked down, then there were five.

Five white snowmen outside the front door,
An icicle fell on one, then there were four.

Four white snowmen standing by the tree,
One slipped and fell apart, then there were three.

Three white snowmen underneath the yew,
One crumbled overnight, then there were two.

Two white snowmen standing in the sun,
One melted right down, then there was one.

One white snowman standing all alone,
Vanished without a trace, then there was none.

John Foster

HIBERNATING HEDGEHOG

Here comes Winter,
cold and grey.
It's time to tuck
myself away.

Here comes ice
and here comes snow.
I need somewhere
warm to go.

Here comes mist
and freezing fog.
Here's a good old
hollow log.

And here's a pile
of leaves that's deep.
I'll roll up here
and go to sleep.

Tony Mitton

GETTING DRESSED FOR WINTER

The actions for this rhyme are simple mimes of the processes described. Demonstrate a specific version for children to copy, or invite the children to think out an appropriate mime for themselves.

Pull on your warm woolly hat.
Nice and tight now.
That's that.

Wrap your neck with a woolly scarf.
If it tickles you —
just laugh!

Put on your coat.
Do it up tight.
That's right.

Here are some socks that are cosy and thick.
Pull them on, quick!

Fetch some warm and waterproof mitts.
See if this pair fits.

Now:
Roll up a snowball,
Pat it with care.
Throw it up high
in the freezing air...

Tony Mitton

RAINBOW RHYME

(to a clapping 'rap' rhythm)

Red and orange and yellow and green
Are the prettiest colours we've ever seen!
But so is blue n' indigo n' violet too!
We think they're <u>all</u> so pretty...
Don't you too?!

Janet Morris and Linda Mort

JACK FROST

Jack Frost came to my garden.
Sing softly. Fingers of one hand
tiptoe the other arm.
He crept here in the night.
He spread his icy fingers
Spread out fingers straight and pointed.
and everything turned white.
Ripple fingers, gently wave arms.

Jack Frost came to my garden.
As before.
He crept here in the night.
The snow fell in the morning
Sprinkling motion with wiggling fingers,
starting with hands held high,
then slowly bringing them down.
and everything turned white.

Jill Atkins

PHOTOCOPIABLE RESOURCES

STORIES

THE FOGGY DAY

There was thick fog in Greendale. Postman Pat had to go slowly along the winding lanes.

'This is nasty,' said Pat.

Jess fluffed up his fur; he didn't like fog either — it made a cold and clinging wetness in the air.

Pat was late when he reached the village post-office. Mrs Goggins was busy dusting the shelves.

'Good morning, Mrs Goggins!' called Pat. 'Sorry I'm late — it's this awful fog.'

'No need to hurry,' said Mrs Goggins. 'There's no sign of the letters yet. The fog's made you late; it will make the letters late, too. Come in and sit down and have a cup of tea.'

Pat went into Mrs Goggin's sitting room, at the back of the shop. There were big armchairs and a blazing fire. Pat warmed his hands and sat back amongst the cushions. Jess curled up near the fire and purred.

'I'll just brew up,' said Mrs Goggins.

'Thank you,' said Pat. 'This is lovely.'

Pat was just getting warm and comfortable, and Mrs Goggins was just bringing the tea and biscuits, when PING went the shop's doorbell.

'It's early for a customer,' said Mrs Goggins.

'That's a good cup of tea,' said Pat. But Mrs Goggins came in with a mail-bag, saying, 'It's here!'

Pat was surprised. 'What, already? Just as I've picked my favourite biscuit, too. No time for that, now. I'd better be on my way. Come on, Jess.'

He went into the shop and helped Mrs Goggins to sort the letters. Then out into the fog again, and Pat was on his way. He knew the Greendale roads well enough but they looked different in the fog.

He went the wrong way somewhere, so he stopped to look at a signpost. But it wasn't a signpost; only a crossroads sign. Now what? Pat didn't know which way to go. He walked along the lane, trying to see where he was.

Then he saw someone standing in the field. He said, 'Why is he so still? It must be Ted Glen, out after rabbits. He'll know the way. I'll pop over with his letter and ask him.'

Pat walked across the field very quietly, so as not to frighten the rabbits away.

He touched Ted on the shoulder.

Ted didn't move.

He put the letter in Ted's pocket.

Still Ted did not move.

He gave Ted a nudge.

Ted swung round suddenly! Oh! It wasn't Ted at all! It was a scarecrow. Pat did feel silly. He said, 'Sorry scarecrow, the letter isn't for you, and I don't suppose you can tell me the way in this fog. Goodbye!'

Pat walked back to the road. He was wondering what to do, when he saw lights coming through the fog. It was Alf Thompson on his tractor. Luckily, he wasn't lost; he soon showed Pat which way to go.

Pat was on his way again. His next stop was at the church. The Reverend Timms met him at the door. He said, 'Hello, Pat. Isn't this fog ghastly! I don't know how you find the way. It's choir practice, too. I expect Miss Hubbard will come; nothing stops her. Three letters today? Thanks, Pat. Now go carefully and trust in the Lord. Goodbye!'

'Cheerio, Reverend.'

When Pat looked in his van, Jess had gone! He looked everywhere – under the van, behind the van, over the wall. There was no sign of Jess. Where could that cat be? He called – 'Jess! Jess!' There was no answer. Perhaps Jess had gone looking for rabbits? Pat set out to seek him.

He called and called and called...

'Jess! Jess! Where are you?' He went over a stile, and across a field; through a gate, through a small wood, into another field, calling all the time, 'Where are you, Jess? Jess! Jess! Come on, Jess. Here, puss; silly puss – this is not time for hide and seek.'

He sat down on a tussock to rest. He put his head on something furry. It moved!

'Oh!' What a fright it gave him. It was Jess! 'Jess, you silly cat. Where have you been?'

Jess was cold and wet; Pat could not be too cross with him. He gave him a cuddle, then tucked him under his arm, saying, 'Come on, Jess. We'd better be on our way. Now, let's see, which way is it?'

Pat was lost again and the fog was thicker than ever.

'Now you've done it, Jess. We're really lost this time.'

Pat began to wander about in the fog. He couldn't find the road, let alone his van. He walked into mud, up to his ankles. Then he stumbled through a stream and a patch of nettles. The branches of a tree scratched his face and knocked his hat off. The fog swirled around him. He was lost, and more surely lost with every step.

Not so very far away, Miss Hubbard was

cycling along the road. When she saw Pat's van she stopped and looked inside.

'No Pat? No Jess?' she said. 'I wonder if they are in the church?'

There was only the Reverend Timms in the church, sorting out the hymn books.

'Hello, vicar,' said Miss Hubbard. 'Have you seen Pat? His van's outside, and there's no sign of him or his cat. Whatever can have happened to them?'

'Dear me,' said the Reverend Timms. 'Pat called some time ago. They must be lost in the fog.'

'I know what we must do,' said Miss Hubbard. 'We must ring the bells to guide them back to the church.'

And that is what they did. They pulled the robes, and the bells clanged and clamoured in the church-tower.

Out in the misty fields, Pat stopped to listen.

'Bells?' he said. 'I thought it was *choir* practice. I wonder what they're ringing for. They're as good as a fog-horn. We'll soon find the way, now.'

Pat followed the sound. The way went through a bramble-patch and some *very* prickly gorse; but it wasn't long before he found the road, then his van, then the church.

The church door opened, and in came Pat, blinking in the light.

'There's Pat!' cried Miss Hubbard, and they stopped ringing.

'Hello,' said Pat. 'It's a good job you rang those bells. We were properly lost. Never mind, we're all right now.'

'The good Lord will be our guide,' said the Reverend Timms. 'Come and have some tea; there's plenty in the pot.'

'Thanks — I need it,' said Pat. There was milk for Jess.

They talked of other foggy days they had known, and enjoyed their tea.

Then, Miss Hubbard said, 'Look at the windows!' The coloured glass was shining quite brightly. 'It's much brighter outside.' They went to the door.

A breeze was blowing the fog away and the sun was beginning to shine. They could see the fields and hills again.

'That's much better,' said Pat. 'Now I can get on with my letters. Come on, Jess. Cheerio! Thanks for the tea!'

Pat waved goodbye and went on his way. It was lovely driving along in the sunshine, without getting lost. They passed the scarecrow, standing patiently in its field. 'Look, Jess,' said Pat. 'That scarecrow's still waiting for a letter.'

Jess was hoping there would be a rabbit pie for tea.

John Cunnliffe

LEROY'S RAINBOW

Leroy's mum had bought him a new storybook. It had a big rainbow on the cover and was all about some people who lived at the end of the rainbow. Leroy loved it. Especially the picture of the rainbow.

'I wish I could see a rainbow,' he said, looking up at the blue sky with it's cotton-wool clouds.

'You'll have to wait for it to rain,' said Mum, taking the wet washing out of the machine. 'You'll only get a rainbow when it's rainy and sunny together.'

'It's sunny today, so if it rains will there be a rainbow?' asked Leroy.

'There could be,' nodded Mum. 'Do you want to help me hang out this washing?'

'Okay!' Leroy picked up the peg bag.

Out in the garden, Leroy looked up at the sky again. He was sure it was getting a bit darker. 'I think it's going to rain,' he said.

'I hope not,' said Mum. 'I've got all this washing to dry.'

A little while later it did rain. 'Hooray!' cheered Leroy.

Mum groaned and they both ran to get the washing in.

Afterwards, Leroy sat by the window watching the rain drizzle down. It was only a short shower and soon stopped. He opened the door, ran out in the garden and eagerly looked up at the sky.

'There isn't a rainbow!' he cried.

'Never mind, there's always another day.'

Leroy was very disappointed. He was still staring miserably out of the window, waiting for it to rain, when his dad came home.

'And what have you been doing today?' asked Dad.

'Waiting for a rainbow,' Leroy told him gloomily, 'but one never came.'

'Well, why don't we *paint* a rainbow?' suggested Dad.

Leroy thought that was a super idea. He ran to get his paints right away.

'Don't forget your apron!' shouted Mum.

Dad covered the table with newspaper. Then he put two big pieces of white paper and Leroy's paints on top of it.

Leroy opened his storybook so he knew what colours to paint the rainbow. Red, orange, yellow, green, blue, indigo and violet. Just like the one in his book.

'That's a smashing rainbow,' said Dad.

'I'm going to put it on my bedroom wall,' said Leroy. 'Right by my bed.'

At bedtime, Mum read Leroy his rainbow storybook again.

'Do you think I'll see a rainbow tomorrow?' he asked.

'Maybe,' said Mum. 'Now, night-night, sleep tight!'

Leroy snuggled down in bed and looked at his rainbow picture on the wall. He looked at it until his eyes closed and he fell asleep.

Pitter, pitter, patter!

The rain splashed down on the window and woke Leroy up. He got out of bed and ran over to the window. It was raining. Absolutely pouring.

He ran excitedly into his parents' bedroom.

'Mum! Dad! Wake up! It's raining! Now I might see a rainbow.'

His parents grunted and went back to sleep. So Leroy returned to his bedroom and watched the rain splashing down. Splish! Splash! Splosh!

It rained all morning. Leroy thought it would never stop. Finally, the clouds lifted.

'Come on, Leroy,' said his mum. 'The rain's stopping now. Let's go shopping.

We can take an umbrella.'

Out in the street, Leroy looked up. The sun was peeping out from behind a cloud and the rain had almost stopped. But he couldn't see a rainbow.

Then he saw it in a puddle on the ground.

'Look, Mum! The rainbow's fallen out of the sky!' he cried. Mum looked at the puddle and laughed.

'That isn't a rainbow, Leroy. Someone's spilt oil from their car and the light makes it look like a rainbow puddle.'

Leroy was relieved!

All the way to the shops he kept looking for a rainbow.

'Leroy, please look where you're going!' Mum said, when he bumped into a lamppost.

'But, Mum. It's stopped raining and there isn't a rainbow!' he cried. 'I'll never see one!'

'Yes you will, look!' said Mum, pointing at the sky behind them.

Leroy turned around. And there it was. A beautiful rainbow, arching over the rooftops and dipping out of sight behind the church.

'Isn't it lovely, Mum?' he gasped. 'Much better than the picture in my book!'

'Much better,' smiled Mum.

Karen King

A BRAVE GIRL

This story begins a long time ago with a tremendous storm blowing in the North Sea, near Northumberland. The wind howled and the waves crashed and a steamship called the Forfarshire ran aground on the Big Harker rocks. The ship sank, but a few survivors managed to swim and clamber up on to the rocks. They sat on the rocks and shivered with cold and shouted for help, but no one heard them.

Meanwhile, in the little bedroom of the Longthorne Lighthouse, a girl called Grace Darling was trying to sleep, near to her father and mother. Grace could hear the howling wind and crashing waves. She tossed and turned but couldn't get to sleep. Suddenly, she thought she could hear the sound of people crying for help. She ran to the window, and heard the cries again, being carried by the wind.

Grace decided to ask her father to take the rowing boat out to try and save the people. Gently, she shook her father's shoulders to wake him up. He shook his head sadly when Grace asked him to take the boat out. He was an old man, and knew

he was not strong enough to row a boat by himself.

Grace put her arm around her father and said she could help him to row the boat. They woke up Grace's Mother, and quickly ran down to the rowing boat, and Grace and her father climbed inside. Grace's mother handed them the oars, and waved goodbye.

Grace and her father rowed as hard as they could. The wind blew harder and louder and blew the sea into great waves which tossed the little boat up and down. Grace and her father thought they would be drowned.

At last, they reached the rocks. Grace kept the boat steady, while her father helped the people into the boat. Then they rowed back to the lighthouse. Grace's mother gave them all some food. A little later, the survivors thanked Grace and her father for saving them and waved goodbye. They told a lot of people what had happened and soon Grace and her parents became very famous.

Linda Mort and Janet Morris

A BRAVE BOY

There is a country called Holland where some of the land is lower down than the sea. Sometimes, the sea can flood the land, so the Dutch people have built tall and strong walls, called dykes, to keep out the sea.

Once, a long time ago, there was a little boy called Peter. One day his mother asked him to take some cakes to an old blind man who lived near the dyke. 'Of course I will,' said Peter, and off he went. He walked along the dyke and could hear the wind blowing the sea into giant waves. 'Oh dear,' thought Peter, 'I hope there isn't going to be a storm tonight.' Peter arrived at the old man's cottage and gave him the cakes. 'Thank you very much, Peter,' said the old man. 'You and your mother are very kind but you must go home quickly now, in case there is a storm.'

Peter began to run home, beside the dyke. By now, the wind was blowing even harder, and it was beginning to rain. Just then, Peter heard a little trickle, trickle, drip, drip, drip. Peter ran to the dyke, and saw a little crack where the sea water was beginning to seep through! 'Oh no! There's a leak in the dyke!' cried Peter. 'Help, Help!' he shouted, but nobody could hear him.

Peter was very, very frightened, but he knew he had to do something. If I run to get help, he thought, then more and more water will get through, and the dyke will crash, and the sea will flood all the land, and people and animals may be drowned! I'll have to try and stop the water coming through! So he began to scoop up handfuls of earth and put it on top of the crack.

He did this all night long, scooping up earth, and shouting for help, but nobody heard him, and nobody came.

At last, in the morning, some farmers found him. Poor Peter was exhausted and very very cold, but he was so pleased that he had stopped the sea from getting through the dyke. The farmers carried Peter home and some others mended the dyke. When everyone heard what had happened, they all cheered and called Peter 'Brave Peter' and thanked him for saving the land from being flooded.

This story was written in 1865 by the American author Mary Dodge.

Simplified and abridged by
Linda Mort and Janet Morris

SONGS

SUMMERTIME

1. I like splash-ing in the sea, I like jump-ing in the waves, I like pad-dling in the pools On a hot, hot sum-mer's day.

2. I like digging in the sand,
I like watching little crabs,
See them hide among the rocks
On a hot, hot summer's day.

Jean Gilbert

SPLISH SPLASH

Splish splash, splish splash, Rain is pour-ing down, Splish splash, splish splash, pud-dles on the ground.

Splish splosh, splish splosh, Play-ing in the rain, Splish splosh, splish splosh, Here we go a-gain.

Carole Henderson-Begg

SNOWY FOOTPRINTS

Capo 3rd fret

1. Some-bo-dy's been out there I know, They've left their foot-prints in the snow.

Who came a-long and where did they go, van-ish-ing off in-to the snow?

See those foot-prints of a paw, They must be those of the cat next door.

2. Somebody's been out there I know,
They've left their footprints in the snow.
Who came along and where did they go
Vanishing off into the snow?
See those footprints of a bird,
It's flown away, it must have heard.

3. Somebody's been out there I know,
They've left their footprints in the snow.
Who came along and where did they go
Vanishing off into the snow?
See those footprints very clear,
They must be the postman's, the post is here!

Make up some more verses.

Jean Gilbert

JUST LIKE THE BIRDS DO

When the Aut - umn ar - rives, Birds on tel - e - phone wires,

All get read - y to fly Ev - er so far a - way.

Let's all fly a - way for the win - ter. Let's all fly to some - where much warm - er.
Let's all fly to dif - fer - ent coun - tries. Let's all fly to some - where where sun is.

Let's all fly a - way for the win - ter just like the birds do.
Let's all fly a - way for the win - ter just like the birds do.

Let's all fly to different countries.
Let's all fly to somewhere where sun is.
Let's all fly away for the winter
just like the birds do.

Clive Barnwell

PHOTOCOPIABLE RESOURCES

SUNSHINE CALYPSO

1. Come from be-hind that cloud, Mis-ter Sun-shine, Come from be-hind that cloud.

I know you're up there, I lnow you're hid-ing, Come from be-hind that cloud.

2. Show me your glowing face, Mister Sunshine
Show me your glowing face.
I know you're up there,
I know you're hiding,
Show me your glowing face.

3. Wake up the world with light, Mister Sunshine.
Wake up the world with light.
I know you're up there,
I know you're hiding,
Wake up the world with light.

Hazel Hobbs

A RAINBOW

Se-ven co-lours mak-ing an arch in the sky, __ When the sun is shin-ing but rain-drops still fly, __

Red, or-ange, yel-low, green and blue, In-di-go and vio-let make a rain-bow for you. __

Sue Nicholls

BLOW WIND BLOW

D   **A**

1. I don't care if the wind may blow, Mov - ing bran - ches to and fro,

D   *Fine*

lift - ing hats then let - ting go, blow a lit - tle hard - er, blow, wind, blow.

G   **A**   *D.C. al Fine*

Make sails bil - low, make flags fly, in - side out go peo - ple's um - b - rel - las.

2. I don't care if the wind may blow,
bringing rain or bringing snow,
lifting kites then letting go,
blow a little harder, blow, wind, blow.

3. I don't care if the wind may blow,
making all those windmills go,
lifting leaves then letting go,
blow a little harder, blow, wind, blow.

Clive Barnwell

A FOGGY DAY

1. It's ve-ry fog-gy to-day,_____ It's ve-ry fog-gy to-day,_____ The

hous-es have van-ished o-ver the way, They've van-ished be-hind a wall of grey, It's

ve-ry fog-gy to-day,_____ It's ve-ry fog-gy to-day._____

> It's very foggy today (repeat)
> The streets don't look the same at all,
> The traffic is moving at a crawl,
> It's very foggy today (repeat).

Sue Nicholls

WHEN THE BLUE SKIES TURN TO GREY

Chorus **Gm**   **D7**

There are grey clouds in the sky, And the blue sky's gone a-way. 1. We

D7   **Gm**

know the rain is com-ing when the blue sky turns to grey.

Further verses

   2. We'll get out our umbrellas etc.
   3. We'll go and find our wellies etc.
   4. We'll take in all the washing etc.

Get out two sets of chime bars:
Set one: notes G, Bb, D. – give one each to a
group of children – these are the GREY group.
Set two: notes D, F#, A, C. – give one each to another
group of children. These are the BLUE group.

Tell the grey group they must play
every time they hear the word 'grey'.
Tell the blue group they must play
every time they hear the word 'blue'.

Jan Holdstock

SAFE SUN

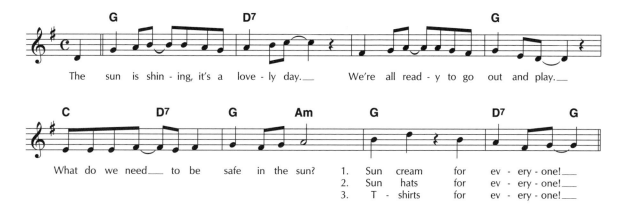

The sun is shin - ing, it's a love - ly day.___ We're all read - y to go out and play.___

What do we need___ to be safe in the sun?
1. Sun cream for ev - ery - one!___
2. Sun hats for ev - ery - one!___
3. T - shirts for ev - ery - one!___

2. The sun is shining, it's a lovely day.
We're all ready to go out and play.
What do we need to be safe in the sun?
Sun hats for everyone!

3. The sun is shining, it's a lovely day.
We're all ready to go out and play.
What do we need to be safe in the sun?
T-shirts for everyone!

Jan Holdstock

THEMES
for early years

Name _____

How many pennies?

◆ Put real pennies on top.

◆ Now cover up the pennies.
Can you still count out the right number?

THEMES
for early years

Name _____

Rain forest tree

This is a tree in the Malaysian rain forest.
◆ Cut out the animals and stick them
where they like to be.

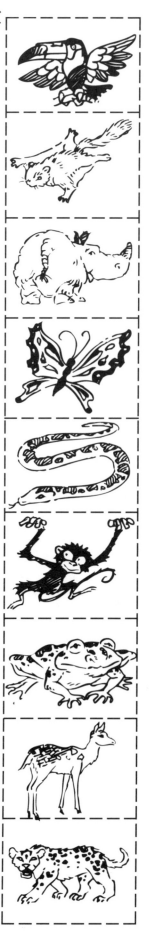

THEMES
for early years

Don't get lost!

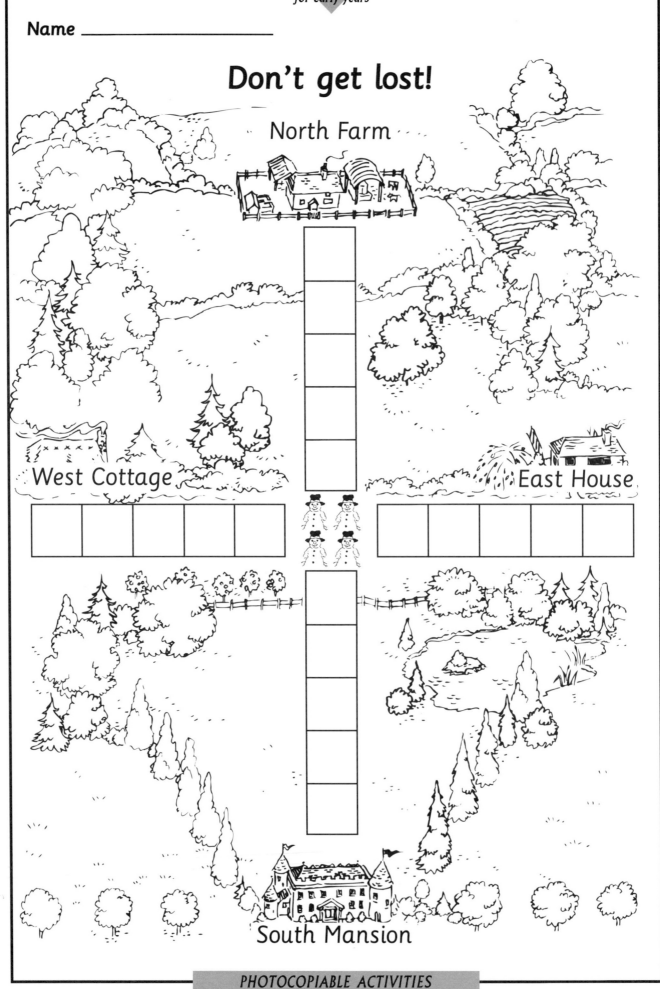

North Farm

West Cottage

East House

South Mansion

THEMES
for early years

Name _____

Traffic jam

◆ Draw sad faces on each of the drivers in
this traffic jam. Why are they sad?

They decide to go to work by bus instead.
◆ Draw their happy faces in the bus
windows. Why are they happy now?

THEMES
for early years

Snowmen

◆ Draw details on the snowmen to make matching pairs.

THEMES
for early years

Name _____

Seasonal trees

Spring

Summer

Autumn

Winter

THEMES
for early years

Name _____

What's the weather like?

◆ Match the weather sign to the right picture.

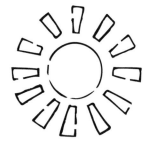

FOG

THEMES
for early years

The right weather

◆ Draw the right weather for each activity.

Name _____

RECOMMENDED MATERIALS

STORY BOOKS
Angry Arthur Hiawyn Oram (Red Fox)
The Big Storm Dave and Julie Saunders
(Frances Lincoln)
Cloudland John Burningham (Jonathan Cape)
The Ducks' Winter Tale Dave and Julie Saunders
(Frances Lincoln)
The Inside Seaside Mavis Taylor (Hutchinson)
Karl's Kite (My first weather book), Hannah
Roche (De Agostini Editions Ltd)
The Lighthouse Keeper's Lunch Ronda
and David Armitage, (Hippo Books)
Little Mo Martin Waddell (Walker Books)
One Snowy Night Nick Butterworth
(Picture Lions)
Pete's Puddle (My first weather book)
Hannah Roche (De Agostini Editions Ltd)
Postman Pat's Foggy Day John Cunliffe
(Hippo Books)
The Snowman Raymond Briggs (Hamish Hamilton)
Storm Boy Paul Owen Lewis (Barefoot Books)
The Tiny Seed Eric Carle, (Hamish Hamilton)
Think of an Eel Karen Wallace, (Walker Books)
What is the Sun? Reeve Lingbergh (Walker Books)
What Will the Weather be Like Today? Paul
Kazuko Roagers (Orchard Books)
Where's Wally? Martin Handford (Walker Books)

INFORMATION BOOKS
Experiment with weather Miranda Bauer
(Two Can Publishing Ltd)
Find Out about Weather Terry Jennings
(BBC Education)
Flood, Julia Waterlow (Wayland)
I Wonder Why the Wind Blows Anita Ganeri
(Kingfisher)
The Weather Series (Wayland)
Storm, Jenny Wood (Wayland)
Weather Watch Series (Franklyn Watts)
Weather Brian Cosgrove (Dorling Kindersley Eye
Witness Guide)
Why Do We Have Wind and Rain? Claire Llewellyn
(Hamlyn)
The Seasons, Topic Box Series Claire Llewellyn
(Hamlyn)
Rain and Shine Paul Rogers (Orchard Books)
Weather, Everyday Science Series (Macdonald
Young Books)

SONG AND POEMS
Earth ways, Earthwise. Poems on Conservation, ed.
Judith Nicholls (Oxford University Press)
*The Harlequin Music Book – 44 Songs for
Around the Year* (A & C Black)
*Twinkle, Twinkle Chocolate Bar. Rhymes for the
Very Young* ed. John Foster (Oxford University
Press)
Poems about weather Amanda Earl and Danielle
Sensier (Wayland)

OTHER RESOURCES
Small bells ('Cat bells'), and small aluminium
and copper shapes, for hanging on wind chimes
are available by mail catalogue from Fred Aldous,
P.O. Box 135, 37 Lever St., Manchester M60 1UX
Sunflower Propagating Kit available from the
Master Herbalist Ltd., Grt. Brickhill,
Bucks MK17 9AQ (send a stamp).

PHOTOCOPIABLE RESOURCES